I doubt there's ever ~~been a more important time for a book that teaches~~ us the art of listening. The rise of tribalism—both in the world and in the church—has made it increasingly difficult for us to really hear one another. If we want things to change, we simply must do better. Thankfully, Brian Davies's new book teaches not only why we should listen but, more importantly, also how to actually do it. I pray we all take its lessons to heart and put them into practice.

Scott Christenson, senior pastor,
St. Paul's Lutheran Church and School, Orange, California

In a world that is always going from one thing to the next, Brian invites us to slow down and be present. Through Scripture and story, he reminds us that if we want to love like Jesus, we should listen like Jesus. *Captivating Conversations* encourages us to create deeper relationships as we reclaim the art of listening. This is a book I wish I had read years ago but am thankful to have it now!

Tanner Olson, poet, speaker,
and author of *Continue: Poems and Prayers of Hope*

If you do not want to be challenged by a book, you should not read this one. Why? It opens the Scriptures, reveals not only the identity of Jesus but also how He engages the people He was sent to save with purposeful questions. You will learn about Jesus from Jesus. Pastor Davies invites us to be more curious about Jesus and one another. You will be challenged to go beyond superficial conversations with better questions and deeper listening. Davies's advice is practical, intentional, down to earth, and given in such a way we can all apply it—I know I will. Every church worker, lay leader, and disciple of Jesus, this book is worthy of your time and attention!

Rev. Dr. Allan R. Buss, president, Northern Illinois District, LCMS

Amid the cacophony of our culture's opposing voices, what if you and I choose to communicate differently? What could happen if we stop speaking divisively or talking over one another; if we pursue personal engagement, longing to listen more than hungering to be heard? What if we ask thoughtful questions with an earnest desire to learn and understand others better? According to Brian Davies, in his insightful and timely new book, bridges can be built, relationships repaired, communities engaged, understanding gained—and more.

In *Captivating Conversations*, receive a perceptive cultural premise regarding the current state of conflict in many of our conversations. Learn from the eye-opening example of Jesus, the master communicator, through His perfect work and words. Jesus' thoughtful questions invite people to draw near, self-reflect, and discover divine truth. Engage in several exercises and receive special techniques that will prepare you (as they have me!) for thoughtful conversations that include purposeful, specific questions to ask others, all while emulating the Savior, by God's grace. You will find yourself reading and referencing this excellent resource again and again!

Deb Burma, Christian speaker and author of several books, including
Joy: A Study of Philippians*; *Leaning on Jesus*; and *Be Still and Know

We've all been there—too quick to speak, too slow to listen, mouths open for inserting feet. Pastor Davies offers a biblically grounded, thoroughly practical corrective to our world of "shout first, ask questions later." Not only will this book help you reclaim the lost art of listening but it will also help you look at life and ministry differently. The caustic vitriol of our fallen and falling humanity can only be effectively countered by the Gospel of Christ and by His forgiven and freed saints who open their sanctified ears to a world in need.

Rev. Dr. Jeffrey Leininger, pastor, First Saint Paul's, Chicago

Brian's writing style is engaging and easy to read, making it a pleasure. The very first chapter immediately addresses an issue we all deal with: polarization. This relevance to our current challenges is sure to resonate with you. We are encouraged to be active listeners. In every chapter, you will find solid biblical teaching, practical examples, and thought-provoking questions to engage you further. This will make a great addition to your personal library and a great book to discuss with church staff and board members.

Rev. Dr. B. Keith Haney, assistant to the president for missions, human care, and stewardship, Iowa District West, LCMS

CAPTIVATING CONVERSATIONS

How Christians Can Reclaim
the Lost Art of Listening

BRIAN K. DAVIES

CONCORDIA PUBLISHING HOUSE · SAINT LOUIS

Published by Concordia Publishing House
3558 S. Jefferson Ave., St. Louis, MO 63118–3968
1-800-325-3040 • cph.org

Manufactured in the United States of America

Library of Congress Cataloging-in-Publication Data

Names: Davies, Brian K., author.

Title: Captivating conversations : how Christians can reclaim the lost art of listening /
Brian K. Davies.

Description: Saint Louis, MO : Concordia Publishing House, [2024] |

Summary: "Information comes at us endlessly from all directions. Our culture promotes
one-sided dialogue, oppositional opinion, and adversarial language—people talking over
and past one another. The result is that the art of listening and value of conversation
are getting lost. This book encourages reflection and introspection and a biblical model
for genuine conversation. It delves into examples and lessons of Jesus so we can, by
the power of the Holy Spirit, reshape the fabric of our lives one conversation at a time"—
Provided by publisher.

Identifiers: LCCN 2024024664 (print) | LCCN 2024024665 (ebook) | ISBN 9780758674340
(paperback) | ISBN 9780758674357 (ebook)

Subjects: LCSH: Listening--Religious aspects--Christianity. | Christian life.

Classification: LCC BV4647.L56 D44 2024 (print) | LCC BV4647.L56 (ebook) | DDC 248.4--
dc23/eng/20240626

LC record available at https://lccn.loc.gov/2024024664

LC ebook record available at https://lccn.loc.gov/2024024665

---

1 2 3 4 5 6 7 8 9 10   33 32 31 30 29 28 27 26 25 24

CONTENTS

INTRODUCTION

IT WAS 2:47 a.m., and my phone was ringing.

Because I serve not only as a pastor to a church but also as a chaplain for a local fire department, I sleep with my phone next to me so I can respond to emergencies. And let me tell you, even though I've had my fair share of middle-of-the-night calls, they still startle me. It often takes my brain a few minutes to wake up and adjust. (Shout-out to the first responders who do this every day!)

This call was from the dispatcher of the fire department. I was being called to a scene. I was provided an address and headed out, knowing very little about what was ahead. I said a prayer while I drove and trusted that the Lord would use me there.

I arrived on the scene, a house where a multigenerational family lived. I was briefed that the matriarch had just passed away. I was asked to provide comfort to the family, which was understandably in shock and distress. As I walked into the house, I thought about my own grandmother, Else, who lived with us until she passed away when I was 13. These are such good memories.

The whole family was packed into the kitchen. Some were sitting at a round table. Others were standing, making an already tight room feel cramped. In the room were two generations: a smattering of children of the woman who had just passed and some of her grandchildren. I introduced myself and quickly determined that there was a language barrier. The oldest English-speaking grandchild, a woman in her early twenties, was my primary point of contact with the family.

And then I made a mistake.

It was early in the morning, remember, and my brain was still waking up. But still, I made a mistake.

After I made brief introductions and expressed words of condolence, I said, "You must have been close to your grandmother." I didn't know that I had stepped into something as the words came out of my mouth, but I sure figured it out when this young woman replied, "No. Actually, we weren't. My grandmother developed dementia in her old age and became very difficult to live with."

Thoughts began running through my mind: *Well, good morning. Regroup. Shift gears. Let's turn this around.*

My mistake in that moment was asking a question that assumed an answer. I projected my own experience onto theirs, believing that life with their grandmother in that home was like mine had been without first learning what their experience was like. And because my assumption was incorrect, it added awkwardness to an already awkward situation. After all, their loved one had just passed away, and a strange guy who spoke a different language was talking to them at their kitchen table.

I quickly began asking questions that assumed no answers. Then I simply listened. I took a posture of curiosity about their matriarch. Over the next hour or so, they shared, mostly through the oldest granddaughter, memories of their grandmother and mother. I heard stories. They cried and laughed as they remembered what life was like before she had dementia. It was really, really neat to hear about their family and spend time with them. At intervals, I felt less like a visitor and more like an observer as they regaled one another with memories. It was a holy moment.

As our conversation neared an end, the oldest granddaughter paused, gathered herself, and shared this incredibly meaningful affirmation with me: "I'm so glad you came to be with us. It means a lot to us that you were here. You're a really good listener." (It appeared that I had recovered from my opening line debacle!)

I share this story to launch this book because, first, it's an example of what's happening all over the place in human relationships—missteps in conversation that create barriers to deeper understanding. Second, it illustrates the power of how being open, curious, and inquisitive builds and strengthens relationships and how that, in turn, establishes a solid foundation for ministry, teaching, and witnessing to the work of Christ in our lives.

For the last few years, I've been on a journey of sorts. I've been observing what's happening in culture, and since you're reading this book, I'm guessing you have as well. Here's what I see: people talking over and at one another, animosity and discord increasing with everyone hopelessly on one side or another. It doesn't feel good, and it for sure doesn't feel *right.*

I've also been on the lookout for moments that seem to be the way things *can* be—times when people seek to understand before seeking to be understood, when people listen without interrupting and ask questions rather than share opinions. I've seen in others and felt in myself the benefits of genuine listening and of being listened to.

I've also come to see that this theme is all over the Bible and central to the ministry of Jesus Christ.

Think about it this way: if there was ever anyone who should walk around and tell people what to do, it was Jesus. Yet many times, that's not what He did. From very early on in His ministry, Jesus employed the art of asking good questions as a means to build bridges with people. I spent some time recording and counting His questions. I also observed that, when people asked questions of Him, Jesus used those moments as opportunities to spark further understanding and inspire curiosity rather than stifle discovery. He asked questions to initiate conversations, point people to God, rebuke His hearers, and test their understanding of Scripture. His questions had purpose.

So let me ask these questions to get you thinking: How many questions do you think Jesus asked in His earthly ministry? How many do you think He Himself answered? (Think about it for a moment.)

You might be surprised to learn that in biblical accounts of His ministry, Jesus asked more than three hundred questions, and He directly answered fewer than ten! Whoa! So, to make a Jesus-like move here and ask some probing questions, what do you make of this? Why do you think Jesus asked so many questions?

The book in your hands explores this.

Our culture promotes one-sided dialogue, combative language, and adversarial conversation. So, instead of following these worldly communication styles, our model for conversation should be the one Jesus gives us. In other words, we should build communication bridges with others so we can develop genuine relationships, elicit mutual respect, earn trust, learn about the vast and complex world our Creator has placed us in, and set our minds on the things of God.

In a world bustling with noise, where information flows endlessly and opinions clash constantly, the art of listening seems to have faded into obscurity. Yet amid the cacophony of voices is a timeless truth, a key to profound understanding and transformative relationships. At the heart of this truth is Jesus, whose approach to communication defied convention and captivated hearts. He, the wisest person to walk the earth, harnessed the might of questions to bridge gaps, awaken souls, and facilitate transformations, all so He might draw people to Himself, "the way, and the truth, and the life" (John 14:6). As we embark on a journey of discovery into the significance of listening and learning, we are poised to uncover the essence of human connection and personal growth to build up our relationships with others and live in harmony with one another as God calls us to do.

Imagine standing on the dusty roads of ancient Galilee as Jesus walks among His disciples and the crowds that gather to hear Him speak. A sense of awe and anticipation fills the air. Jesus' words, delivered with divine power and wisdom, resonate deeply with His listeners because they are the very words of God. His monologues are recorded in Scripture to leave a lasting impression on us today.

Jesus' use of questions set Him apart as a communicator of unparalleled caliber. As we explore the depth of His interactions, we find that His questions were not merely techniques for eliciting information; they were pathways to the human heart, gateways to introspection, and catalysts for profound change. Jesus used dialogue that invited others to reflect, engage, and discover divine truth. His inquiries stirred the intellect and kindled the spirit, sparking conversations that transcended the surface and delved into the core of existence.

Beautifully and masterfully, Jesus asked questions that invited people to confront their own realities—their sinful nature and inability to do anything about it on their own. Through these interactions, He not only revealed His own divine knowledge and wisdom but He also opened the door and created space for transformation through the power of the Holy Spirit.

Jesus' conversational approach was already evident in His childhood, as described in the Gospel of Luke. At the age of 12, He engaged the teachers in the temple with questions that astonished and impressed them. This pattern of using questions as a means of facilitating dialogue and learning would continue throughout His ministry, leaving an indelible mark on His followers and the generations that followed.

As we examine Jesus' words in the Bible, we must confront pressing questions about our own approach to conversation: How often do we prioritize listening? In a world entranced by rapid-fire information, do we pause to truly hear the voices around us? Are we engaging in conversations that encourage reflection, empathy, and growth?

The power of questions lies not only in their ability to unravel the mysteries of others—their thoughts, attitudes, perspectives, and motives—but also in their potential to break down barriers and unlock doors in order to reshape our communities, strengthen our relationships, and transform our perspectives. By adopting a posture of genuine openness and curiosity, we open the way to understanding viewpoints that differ from our own. We become active participants in communication, weaving threads of connection that transcend barriers and biases.

This book exists to help us reclaim the art of listening, to revive the power and potential of asking questions that cut through the noise and touch the soul. Imagine the impact we can create when we use questions to uplift those we love, encourage our neighbors, and foster a climate of open dialogue in our communities. The possibilities are many—strengthened relationships, a more connected society, and a more profound understanding of our shared human journey. This is surely a God-pleasing effort to engage with, and, by the power of the Holy Spirit, we can!

Dear reader, as we embark on this exploration into the art of listening, learning, and questioning, let us embrace the legacy of the ultimate communicator and relationship-builder, Jesus. As we'll see, our Savior beautifully models a healthy posture we can and should take with others. Let us challenge ourselves to be mindful of the questions we ask and the manner in which we listen. Let us recognize that every conversation, by the power of the Holy Spirit, holds the potential to ignite a spark of change, not only in others but also within ourselves.

In the chapters that follow, we will delve deeper into the art of questioning, explore techniques to enhance our interactions, inspire introspection, and foster growth. Through anecdotes, insights, and practical exercises, we will uncover how listening and engaging with intention can pave the way for deeper relationships and the enrichment of our communities. We'll see how Jesus does this and how we can follow His commands to love God above all and to love others as we love ourselves.

Imagine a world where disagreements are opportunities for understanding, where conversations are vehicles for growth, and where questions are the keys to unlocking profound insights. Such a world is not a fantasy; it is a possibility within our reach. Through the potent blend of listening and questioning, we, through the power of the Holy Spirit, have the potential to reshape our communities, one conversation at a time.

So are you ready to embark on this journey of discovery? Are you prepared to explore the treasures of understanding and connection? Let's take this journey together, for within the art of listening and learning lies an important secret that can revolutionize our lives and our world.

Here's the overview of what's in your hands.

The first part is a survey of the landscape around us and Jesus' approach to communication. The second part is a practical look at how listening well is not just a series of skills; it's a mindset shift and an attitude and posture we take toward others.

Putting this attitude into practice will result in you being a better listener, having richer and more meaningful conversations, and developing stronger and healthier relationships. Even better, these practices may heal strained relationships, introduce people to Jesus, and draw others closer to Him.

Here's a quick word on how I've structured this book and why.

Captivating Conversations: How Christians Can Reclaim the Lost Art of Listening is a series of short chapters divided into four sections. (As a reader, I find that shorter chapters are easier to digest.) You can read this book from the beginning straight through to the end. Or you can read the chapters that appeal to you and your situation in the moment, and then go back to read the chapters you skipped at another time.

In fact, let me be so bold as to say this: if you actually want to start by reading sections III and IV, then go back and read I and II, this book will still make sense. It will kind of be like starting with the main story and then diving into the prequel!

Whichever way you choose to read it, I recommend reading this book with other people. We are wired and created by God for community, and if you read this with others, you can discuss and practice together the habits and skills I propose. If you are reading this book as part of a book club or a small group, I recommend meeting several times throughout the reading. Each chapter includes questions for conversation and reflection. The more time you take with the chapters and questions, the more you will process the content, internalize it, and apply it. So please accept my invitation to slow down. The goal of *Captivating Conversations* isn't merely to finish; the goal is to get something out of it that impacts and blesses your life and relationships. Discussing and reflecting on the questions in this book will facilitate that.

However you read this book—on your own or with a group, straight through or by changing the order of the chapters—may this book enrich your relationships and move you to listen more closely to God's Word.

Happy reading (and listening)!

PART I

Hey, Culture. How's It Going?
(There Has to Be a Better Way)

CHAPTER
1

Why do you call Me "Lord, Lord," and not do what I tell you?

JESUS; LUKE 6:46

BRITTANY HAD HAD ENOUGH

LET'S START THIS chapter with a few questions. From what we've just learned in the introduction, this is what Jesus would do, right? So here goes:

- 🗨 How would you describe the level of discourse among humans in our culture these days?

- 🗨 What do you observe as people interact with one another?

Think about these questions for a moment. As you do, here's a quick story:

Brittany cuts my hair, and she is awesome. I wish you could meet her. She's talented, thoughtful, and kind. She's also a good listener; after all, when it's your vocation to be a stylist, you learn how to interact with clients. But by late fall of 2020, she had had enough. I couldn't tell by her disposition toward me and my family (she remained positive and cheerful), but I could tell by the glass jar in her salon with a label that read, "If you say the words *COVID*, *mask*, or *vaccine*, put $20 in this jar." After months of hearing clients riff on these subjects, Brittany wanted to talk about something else.

My observation is that many of us feel like Brittany these days. We've had enough of debating, talking over one another, and feeling like we just can't agree. And I'm not just talking about how the world should have (or could have) handled the pandemic, but about how the world should handle anything—the economy, the political landscape, guns, books, whether the toilet paper unrolls from under the roll or from the top.

Our culture has become increasingly *polarized* and *tribal*. There seems to be little room for nuance, little room for a moderate, middle-ground approach to mediating complex issues. Like the positive and negative terminals on a battery, people are on opposite sides and seem unable, or unwilling, to come together.

This results in heightened levels of *tribalism*. The word *tribalism* describes people interacting with or being in relationship with only those who think like them. Additionally, those within the tribe celebrate being in contempt of "the other" and view people outside their tribe as threats. Tribalism leaves little room for healthy discourse, listening, curiosity, collaboration, and learning.

We see this on both macro and micro levels. On a macro level, we see tribalism in our political and cultural leaders. It's the air we breathe. It's all around us. It seems unavoidable. On a micro level, tribalism is in our relationships, workplaces, churches, and even around our kitchen table. The memes and late-night television jokes about family meals being things to avoid because of divergent political or social views may make us chuckle, but they may also cause us to mourn.

I'm guessing you've seen this in action. As I was writing this, I observed a battle on a social media platform that turned ugly. The debate was heated, the personal attacks were flying, the discourse was in the alley. The topic? Dan Marino's rank on the list of all-time National Football League quarterbacks! Just to clarify, a debate about an athlete who played during the 1980s was drawing visceral, personal attacks.

The reason I bring this up is that it's important to get a read on where we are—to understand the times and know the landscape so we can set a course for moving forward. And the bottom line is this: we are not listening well. In fact, we are doing quite the opposite. We're talking (shouting!) over and around one another. And it's really difficult to listen when you're shouting. Please read that sentence again: *It's really difficult to listen when you're shouting.*

So how did we get here? What's causing this? To get to a solution, to get to "a still more excellent way" (1 Corinthians 12:31), it's important to understand the root causes of it all. Here's how I see it:

WHAT WE'RE CONSUMING

What would your response be if I told you that for a few hours every day, I invite someone into my life to talk over me, yell at me, tell me who to hate, what to fear, and give me generally bad news about the world? What would you say to me? Perhaps it would be something like this:

"You might want to think about that; it's not a good idea to let all that negativity in your life."

I agree. But isn't that what we do every day by allowing cable news pundits and social media celebrities to be such a part of our lives? No wonder so many of us are reporting heightened levels of anxiety!

In the Gospel of Luke, Jesus shares this powerful truth:

The good person out of the good treasure of his heart produces good, and the evil person out of his evil treasure produces evil, for out of the abundance of the heart his mouth speaks. (LUKE 6:45)

Beautifully and powerfully, Jesus says that what resides within us flows outward in our words, gestures, and actions. It makes sense, then, that because our sinful hearts lead us to consume a steady diet of argumentative discourse, negativity, misinformation, and verbal attacks on others, such things regularly and normatively come out of us.

And how much are we consuming? Recent research from a variety of sources says that the average American spends seven hours and three minutes looking at a screen every day. Some quick math on that reveals that we spend almost half of our waking hours looking at screens.[1] Ouch! And lest we say, "Well, some of that screen time is part of my job," statistics from DataReportal reveal that the majority of our screen time is spent on our smartphones. The study says we use our phones to access social media primarily.[2] Again, ouch!

Consider not only the quantity of what is being consumed but the quality. From political talk shows with one-sided spokespersons to raving podcasters to sports shows with guests debating hot topics to viral videos, a common theme binds them: winning the argument, embarrassing the opposition, and "owning" the other.

Here's my point: *The approach taken to get the most likes or shares rarely, if ever, works to build and strengthen relationships.* What works on the internet to get ratings and revenue might not be the best strategy to use at the next gathering with your extended family! A proven and winsome approach is marked by a posture and attitude of openness, curiosity, and asking good, thoughtful, sincere questions. Are you seeing any of that on cable news or social media?

HOW WE'RE CONSUMING IT

One of my favorite parts of my vocation as a parish pastor is visiting homebound folks in our church family. These are people who, for varying reasons, don't leave home very often, so I regularly get to bring God's Word to them and administer to them the Lord's Supper. These are some of my favorite days because the pace of these visits is slow and the conversations are rewarding. I go with the hope of being a blessing to them and depart as the blessed one.

During these visits, there's no need to rush. Conversations take their own pace. I learned from experience that when offered coffee, I should accept it. There is something about clutching a warm beverage that signals to the other person, "Let's slow down a bit." I love these moments; my life needs more of them. Maybe yours does as well.

Time spent visiting a homebound church member is the opposite of time spent on social media. While one is about patience and organic storytelling, the other is about speed and optimized communication. How quickly can you say it? How succinct can you be? Can you stay within the character limit?

In my previous book, *Connected to Christ: Overcoming Isolation through Community*, I shared an observation that's worth sharing again:

> Major health insurance provider Cigna recently completed a survey of more than twenty thousand adults in the United States, and their findings were alarming. Part of the data broke down feelings of isolation and loneliness across different generations and age groups. Before I share the results, think for a moment—which demographic group would you expect to be the loneliest? I would have expected that older generations would report these feelings the most. After all, they often live alone, and we might not think of them as being in the socially prime season of life. However, the Cigna study reported the oldest generation experienced the greatest sense of connection and well-being.

Each subsequent generation felt increasingly lonely and isolated. Gen Z (those born from the mid-to-late 1990s to the early 2010s) reported the most loneliness and isolation.

So think about this: those who are most digitally connected feel the most alone.[3]

My observation, and perhaps you'll agree, is that people who are part of the older generations are good at interpersonal conversation and embracing the moment. The congregation I serve hosts a catered luncheon for our senior members twice a year. We have a summer barbecue and a Christmas luncheon, and both are packed. Folks start to arrive around 11:30 a.m. By noon, our ample church lobby is packed, and the conversation and laughter are already flowing. These are some of my favorite events. Sometimes, I just stand back and watch them all visit. It comes so naturally to them. Even though the food we provide is really, really good, the people are in no rush to eat. Often, we wait thirty to forty-five minutes to serve the meal because we don't want to interrupt the conversation and community building!

These luncheons, however, stand in stark contrast to what we're observing in the rest of the world around us. When we combine the declining nature of our discourse as humans with the means by which this discourse is delivered, it's no wonder we struggle to listen!

So let me ask again the question that kicked off this part of the book: *Hey, culture. How's it going?* I'm guessing you'll agree that we can do better. While the internet and the age of social media have brought unique challenges, they are part of the bigger, age-old problem of our fallen human nature that the Bible speaks to frequently. Good news alert! The Bible points to a better way. In the following chapters, we'll explore this. But first, here are some questions for you to reflect on.

QUESTIONS FOR
CONVERSATION AND REFLECTION

- How would you describe the current level of discourse among people in our culture?

- Where is our culture becoming increasingly polarized?

- Where do you see tribalism happening around you?

- Do you see tribalism in both macrocultures and microcultures? How?

- Think about the following statement: "The approach taken to get the most likes or shares rarely, if ever, works to build and strengthen relationships." Do you agree or disagree? Why?

- How does faith in Jesus Christ invite us into something better?

- How does being a Christian invite us to think of others differently?

- Read 1 Peter 3:8. How does this verse inform your view of the world today?

CHAPTER
2

Can a blind man lead a blind man? Will they not both fall into a pit?

JESUS; LUKE 6:39

AN AGE-OLD PROBLEM

WHEN WE SEE all the change happening around us, it's tempting to think that what we discussed in chapter 1 is a modern-day experience. It's easy to blame the avalanche of change on the advent of the internet, the influence of cable TV, and the saturation of social media.

The Bible, however, reveals that these things are simply the latest symptoms and manifestations of a much older and deeper issue. Let's look at this together, because to get to the best resolution to the conflict, we have to truly understand the core of the issue before us.

The theme of the Old Testament book of Proverbs is wisdom—what it is and how to acquire it. Here's how Martin Luther describes Proverbs:

> It may properly be called a book of good works, for in it he teaches how to live a good life before God and the world. . . . He puts his teaching into proverbs, so that it can be grasped the more easily and kept the more readily. Anyone . . . might well take this as a handbook or prayerbook for

his daily use, read it often, and ponder his
own life in it.[4]

The bottom line from Luther is that if you want to live
wisely, then live out Proverbs.

The contrast between the wise man and the fool is
central to the book of Proverbs. What they do and say
is examined and held up to us as an example of what to
follow or not follow. If you are familiar with the children's
magazine *Highlights*, it's akin to the Goofus and Gallant
comic strip. The comic contrasts Gallant's actions as right
and Goofus's as wrong.

According to Proverbs 18:2, "A fool takes no pleasure in
understanding, but only in expressing his opinion." Wisdom
involves seeking understanding before airing opinions.
Said another way, wisdom is seeking to understand before
seeking to be understood. This verse tells us that this was
a problem that needed to be addressed millennia ago, in
an entirely different cultural context, on the other side
of the planet. Simply put, it's an age-old, sinful human
nature problem.

Ecclesiastes is another Old Testament book of wisdom.
Written by King Solomon, Ecclesiastes is thought to be
his reflections on all he learned over the course of his
life. In a way, it's like having a cup of bold coffee with a
homebound senior and listening as he or she reflects on
life. I have done that countless times, and let me tell you,
those conversations are powerful! The difference is that
Ecclesiastes is divinely inspired, written by God, and
without error.

One motif repeated in the book of Ecclesiastes is the contrast between talking a lot and remaining silent and listening well. Here's an example:

Be not rash with your mouth, nor let your heart be hasty to utter a word before God, for God is in heaven and you are on earth. Therefore let your words be few. For a dream comes with much business, and a fool's voice with many words. (ECCLESIASTES 5:2-3)

Take note that the Bible is again telling us what we would do well to pay attention to—being "rash with your mouth" and using many words are folly. Wisdom is being measured and thoughtful with your words. I cannot help but think of the timeless quote based on Ecclesiastes 5:2–3:

Better to remain silent and thought a fool than to speak and remove all doubt.

Fast-forward to the New Testament, where James, the brother of our Lord Jesus, builds upon Ecclesiastes 5:2–3:

Know this, my beloved brothers: let every person be quick to hear, slow to speak. (JAMES 1:19)

Generally speaking, when the Bible tells us to "know this," we should pay close attention. So what should we pay close attention to or take note of? Being "quick to hear, slow to speak."

Let those words soak in for a moment. Then ask yourself if you are more likely to be quick to hear or quick to speak. If you're like me, and probably like many other people you know, you will find you are usually too quick to speak, especially in the heat of the moment when the words are bubbling within you and you just can't help but let them out.

As you reflect on those instances, are you proud of them? Or are they moments you wished you had back? I'm speculating that you'd like a do-over.

Recently, on a Monday morning following a busy weekend, I woke up with good intentions: I was going to make breakfast for my family. I headed to the kitchen and grabbed a dozen eggs from the refrigerator. But as I grabbed them, I took hold of only the top half of the carton. As I pulled them out of the fridge, the bottom half (you know, where the eggs are) fell with a great splat. So, to recap, it's early Monday morning, and I'm cleaning a dozen broken eggs off the floor.

The eggs were symbolic of my broken good intentions, and I wasn't handling it well. When my family came down to prepare to leave for the day, they were met by a grumpy, frustrated dad and husband who expressed some words I'd like to have back. Can you identify with this?

Knowing this, knowing the reality of our broken, sinful nature, we also know that the Bible offers a better path forward: "Be quick to hear, slow to speak."

We're not the first to wrestle with this. In fact, we're in good company with Jesus' disciples. I've heard Peter, often the spokesperson for the disciples, described as "the disciple with the foot-shaped mouth" because he regularly spoke without thinking. Peter, a work in progress like each of us, was quick to speak and slow to hear.

On one occasion, Jesus told His disciples what would soon come in His life, and Peter, likely impulsively and without reflection, wanted no part of it:

And He began to teach them that the Son of Man must suffer many things and be rejected by the elders and the chief priests and the scribes and be killed, and after three days rise again. And He said this plainly. And Peter took Him aside and began to rebuke Him. But turning and seeing His disciples, He rebuked Peter and said, "Get behind Me, Satan! For you are not setting your mind on the things of God, but on the things of man." (MARK 8:31-33)

I picture Peter going home after that and his wife asking, "Hi, honey. How was your day at work?" Then Peter's reply: "Well, Jesus called me Satan. But other than that, it was great!"

And why? All because Peter was slow to hear, slow to process, but quick to speak!

Mark's Gospel reports a similar episode shortly thereafter. It's the transfiguration moment, when Peter, James, and John are taken up to a high mountain and Jesus is transfigured before them. The Bible records it going down like this:

And He was transfigured before them, and His clothes became radiant, intensely white, as no one on earth could bleach them. And there appeared to them Elijah with Moses, and they were talking with Jesus. (MARK 9:2-4)

Now, the question becomes, What would the disciples make of this? How would they respond? Mark tells us that it's quintessential Peter:

And Peter said to Jesus, "Rabbi, it is good that we are here. Let us make three tents, one for You and one for Moses and one for Elijah." *For he did not know what to say.* (MARK 9:5-6, EMPHASIS ADDED)

The Bible records that Peter didn't know what to say! (This detail strikes me as funny.) Frankly, I don't blame him; the transfiguration was surely a sight to behold. Yet still, he opens his mouth and starts talking! He's one of us! Check out what God does next:

And a cloud overshadowed them, and a voice came out of the cloud, "This is My beloved Son; *listen to Him.*" And suddenly, looking around, they no longer saw anyone with them but Jesus only. (MARK 9:7-8, EMPHASIS ADDED)

So, to sum it up, the wisdom of God is more listening, less talking—specifically, more listening to Jesus, following the Lord's lead, guidance, and direction, and less off-the-cuff responding without thinking.

This account can give people like you and me hope that when we find ourselves quick to speak and slow to listen, we are not alone and have good company. What we see in our culture is not a modern internet- and social-media-fueled problem. It's an original sin problem and one that this account in Mark reveals that the disciples faced too.

Enter Jesus.

In the following chapters, we will dive into two seismic truths woven together. First, we'll see the identity of Jesus as our Savior. He is God incarnate. He came to be among us and to live a perfect life, only to be mocked, beaten, and crucified, laying down His life as the ultimate sacrifice to atone for the sins of the world in order to reconcile us to our Creator in fulfillment of prophecy. That's who He is and what He did for us.

We'll also see the identity of Jesus as the one who listens. This is an extension of His ministry as our servant Savior. In a beautiful act of love and service, our Messiah not only saves us but also cares enough to listen to us. We'll see the ways He intentionally chose to interact with others. We'll see Him ask a lot of questions, and we'll see Him as the one who is perfectly "quick to hear, slow to speak." In doing so, we'll see Him not only strengthening relationships and increasing understanding but also modeling for us an approach for human interaction that is sorely needed today.

Are you ready? Let's go!

QUESTIONS FOR
CONVERSATION AND REFLECTION

🗨 Do you observe people delighting in airing their own opinions? Why do you think they do this?

🗨 Do you catch yourself delighting in airing your own opinions? What circumstance or topic usually gets you going? Why do you think that is?

🗨 Why is it difficult to be "quick to hear, slow to speak"?

🗨 Where and when do you most often say that you'd like to have something back (at home, at work, with friends, and so on)?

🗨 Who in your life listens well? What leads him or her to be a good listener?

🗨 Read Luke 8:21. How does this verse impact your view of the world today?

PART II

Divine Whispers, Profound Revelations

CHAPTER 3

Why were you looking for Me?
Did you not know that I must be
in My Father's house?

JESUS; LUKE 2:49

IT STARTED EARLY

HAVE YOU EVER wondered what Jesus was like as a teenager?

It's a question I hear from time to time. What was Jesus really like as a child? a preteen? a teenager? It's hard to imagine a teenager who doesn't have mood swings and who handles all of his or her responsibilities impeccably and never talks back, right? We know He was perfect. He was the sinless Son of God, after all. So how does a *perfect* teenager act?

We're curious about Jesus' life, so it's disappointing that God intentionally gives us only one biblical account of His early days. Let that sink in. From the time soon after He was born through the time He publicly launched His ministry, we have only one glimpse into what Jesus was like growing up. One.

> Give the teens in your life an extra measure of grace. *It's been difficult to be a teenager in every century, but it's particularly difficult these days!*

Let's set the scene. Jesus is twelve years old. As part of their religious practice, his parents make a yearly journey to Jerusalem for Passover. After celebrating, it's time for them to return home. They begin the trek home, only to discover they are without their son! They search for Him among their traveling company and along the road back to Jerusalem. After three days (three days!), they find Him. He had remained in Jerusalem. It's like the Bible's version of the 1990 movie classic *Home Alone*.

So where would you expect Jesus to be in Jerusalem? Where would you look for a twelve-year-old boy in a big city? The marketplace? The playground where other boys might be?

And when they did not find Him, they returned to Jerusalem, searching for Him. After three days they found Him in the temple, sitting among the teachers, listening to them and asking them questions. And all who heard Him were amazed at His understanding and His answers. And when His parents saw Him, they were astonished. And His mother said to Him, "Son, why have You treated us so? Behold, Your father and I have been searching for You in great distress." And He said to them, "Why were you looking for Me? Did you not know that I must be in My Father's house?" (LUKE 2:45–49)

There's just so much we can draw from this, but for our purposes, let's zero in on one aspect: not only where Jesus is but *what* He's doing.

First, He's in the temple (again, not a place you'd expect to find a typical twelve-year-old boy). But in addition, and most important, He's "sitting among the teachers, listening to them and asking them questions."

As noted above, this is the only event the Bible records about Jesus' childhood—or for the roughly thirty years following His birth. Of all the things that likely happened during Jesus' upbringing, why this one?

Notice how Jesus listens to the teachers and then asks insightful questions that amaze them. He does this in the midst of the most intimidating people in His religious community: the leaders of the temple in Jerusalem. This conversation has become a hallmark and centerpiece of what the Bible tells us about how Jesus interacted with others. He asked really good, thoughtful, relationship-building questions. His questions were meant to drive people to the Scriptures, invite people to look closely at what God reveals there, draw them into conversation, help them discover something new about themselves and about God, stimulate reflection and thought, and so much more. This started when He was 12. Throughout His earthly ministry, it was a primary means by which He worked to bring people closer to Him.

I'm not sure if you caught it in the account of Jesus in the temple, but even Jesus' response to His parents when they ask, "Why have You treated us so?" brings about more questions:

And He said to them, "Why were you looking for Me? Did you not know that I must be in My Father's house?" (LUKE 2:49)

Fascinating! In asking His parents these questions, He invites them to consider what they know to be true of

His identity. Both Mary and Joseph had received divine messengers at the time of Mary's pregnancy that revealed the identity of their child—they knew who He was. Jesus' questions foster and facilitate reflection in His parents—a method much more powerful than scolding or belittling. These questions, even if they are succinct and direct, are more powerful than "Mom and Dad, remember that I'm the Messiah! I have to be here! You should know better!"

The rest of that account tells us that Jesus continued to grow and learn and was obedient to His parents. Although it isn't stated, we can infer that Jesus learned by continuing to ask questions.

Early in His earthly ministry, soon after calling His first disciples (see Luke 5:1–11), we are told of a dramatic scene where Jesus uses powerful questions to spur reflection and reveal His identity. Let's review:

It's a packed house—there is barely room to move—because Jesus is in town. Religious leaders from all over, "every village of Galilee and Judea and from Jerusalem" (v. 17), are in the crowd. They have all come to hear Jesus speak and teach. Some men arrive, carrying a paralyzed friend on a mat who they hope can be healed by Jesus. But the crowd is too dense for them to get into the house. That's not the end of the story, as we know.

In the most MacGyver-like move in the New Testament, they climb to the roof of the home, probably using the staircase on the outside of the building, and remove some of the roofing tiles. With a hole exposed, they lower their friend down into the home, right in front of Jesus. Luke records that when Jesus sees their faith, He proclaims to the paralytic, "Man, your sins are forgiven you" (Luke 5:20).

Next, the Pharisees and teachers of the Law begin grumbling and muttering to themselves, questioning Jesus' ability to make such a statement. Check out Jesus' response:

> **When Jesus perceived their thoughts, He answered them, "Why do you question in your hearts? Which is easier, to say, 'Your sins are forgiven you,' or to say, 'Rise and walk'? But that you may know that the Son of Man has authority on earth to forgive sins"—He said to the man who was paralyzed—"I say to you, rise, pick up your bed and go home." And immediately he rose up before them and picked up what he had been lying on and went home, glorifying God. And amazement seized them all, and they glorified God and were filled with awe, saying, "We have seen extraordinary things today." (LUKE 5:22-26)**

Again, from early in His earthly ministry, Jesus exercised a pattern and approach He would often take: ask questions to spur reflection, reveal His identity, and—through the power of the Holy Spirit—draw people to Himself. Let's go deeper.

This is, no doubt, a tense scene. The room is packed, and many skeptical eyes are fixed on Jesus. After Jesus declares that the paralyzed man's sins are forgiven, the scoffing of the religious leadership amplifies. Knowing the condition of their hearts and wanting everyone present to see Him for who He truly is, Jesus lowers the temperature in the room, tension-wise, by asking a question that invites everyone in the room to think about what is going on: "Which is easier, to say, 'Your sins are forgiven you,' or to say, 'Rise and walk'?"

This question has only one answer: neither! Both are impossible—for a mortal, that is. Only God can forgive and heal.

In this highly-charged, dramatic scene, Jesus leads people to conclude that God is present among them. And rather than simply telling them that, His questions invite them to arrive at this fact on their own. Genius.

The questions keep coming. In Luke 6, it's the Sabbath day, and Jesus enters the synagogue. While teaching, Jesus notices a man with a withered right hand. Take note of how Jesus handles this moment:

> **[Jesus] said to the man with the withered hand, "Come and stand here." And he rose and stood there. And Jesus said to them, "I ask you, is it lawful on the Sabbath to do good or to do harm, to save life or to destroy it?" And after looking around at them all He said to him, "Stretch out your hand." And he did so, and his hand was restored. But they were filled with fury and discussed with one another what they might do to Jesus.** (LUKE 6:8-11)

Why do you think Jesus invited the man to come to the front of the group and then asked the group what should be done? Why didn't He just heal the man?

Think of all the deliberating that question sparked in the hearts and minds of those assembled in the synagogue that day. I suspect that it got them thinking about how they understood the Sabbath, what was acceptable or not acceptable on the holy day, and the ordering of priorities between honoring the Sabbath and helping others—both of which were requirements, according to Jewish law.

Jesus asked a question to get them to a new understanding. In His wisdom, He knew that the best way to get them there was not by telling them but by asking a question that sparked reflection on God's Law (as opposed to man-made law). Through the power of the Holy Spirit at work in them, He deepened their understanding of who was present with them—God the Son, who had authority over heaven and earth. What's more, Jesus was observing God's Law by keeping the Sabbath, and He was showing compassion to someone in need, which the religious leaders who were present did not do.

Are you starting to see how powerful simple questions can be? It's worthwhile to pause here for just a moment to reflect on why Jesus took this approach, to consider what is underneath all this.

First, let's address some potential misconceptions. Jesus didn't ask questions because He did not know the answers. Jesus is, after all, true God and therefore omniscient, meaning that He knows all things. So He did not ask questions for the reasons we sometimes do—because we don't know something. And Jesus didn't employ questions because He was waffling or vacillating between options, as though His questions weren't driving toward a lesson. His questions were not of the indifferent "I don't know. What do you want to do?" variety.

Just the opposite. Jesus wants to transform the hearts, minds, souls, and lives of His creation, His people. In His wisdom, because He knows His people better than they know themselves, Jesus is aware that thoughtful questions are efficacious and successful. Questions are the means and tools He employs to take people from where they are to where He desires to get them. His teaching is at the same time deliberate, calculated, and strategic.

And the foreseen end is clear: "For the Son of Man came to seek and to save the lost" (Luke 19:10). Jesus' questions are intended to help us learn that He is "the Son of Man" (see messianic prophecies such as Daniel 7:13–14) who came "to seek and to save the lost." May I implore you, reader, to slow down and take note of who Jesus here declares Himself to be.

He is our Savior who seeks us. He doesn't wait for people to come to Him, to get their lives in order, to clean themselves up before they can have a relationship with Him. No, quite the opposite. Our *seeking* Savior is God, who pursues us and doesn't give up on us no matter how many times we give up on Him. This is who He is, and it's why He came.

Jesus' heart for His people is emphasized three times in the Gospel of Matthew:

> When He saw the crowds, He had *compassion* for them, because they were harassed and helpless, like sheep without a shepherd. (MATTHEW 9:36, EMPHASIS ADDED)

> When He went ashore He saw a great crowd, and He had *compassion* on them and healed their sick. (MATTHEW 14:14, EMPHASIS ADDED)

> Then Jesus called His disciples to Him and said, "I have *compassion* on the crowd because they have been with Me now three days and have nothing to eat. And I am unwilling to send them away hungry, lest they faint on the way." (MATTHEW 15:32, EMPHASIS ADDED)

This is the heart of the Lord for His people. He has compassion on us, and that compassion leads Him to act. Rather than merely feeling it, He *does* something about it. He seeks and saves.

The apostle Paul put it this way:

> For our sake He made Him to be sin who knew no sin, so that in Him we might become the righteousness of God. (2 CORINTHIANS 5:21)

This is, simply put, the greatest trade in human history. He trades our sin for our salvation. By His sacrifice on the cross and resurrection from the dead, we have peace with God now and life eternal. The perfect life and obedient death of Jesus Christ provides you and me with the gift of salvation. And He sought us out to make it all happen.

His earthly ministry, then, is dedicated to revealing this identity to His first-century audience and us. He has made Himself known, both by how He lives and by how He willingly laid down His life in exchange for ours. John 12:32 says that His death on the cross has had an astounding saving effect:

> **And I, when I am lifted up from the earth, will draw all people to Myself.**

He is the Messiah, the one sent by God to redeem all of mankind, and He wants to make this salvation known to everyone. One of the ways He did this was to ask thoughtful and strategic questions to invite people to hear, see, and fully comprehend for themselves who He is.

It really rocks my world when I think about it this way: no one knows human nature and the human mind better than Jesus. His divine nature means He is one with the Father and is omniscient. His flesh and blood experiences mean He knows our human nature, physical life, and mind. Of all the methods He could have used to teach us, at the top of the list was asking questions.

The bottom line is that if this is the technique and tack of Jesus, we would do well to pay attention to it and use it ourselves. Yet before we consider how we might follow the example of our Teacher, Jesus, let's look at other occurrences of this approach in His earthly ministry. Let's keep going!

QUESTIONS FOR
CONVERSATION AND REFLECTION

- What do you make of Jesus "sitting among the teachers, listening to them and asking them questions" as a twelve-year-old boy in Luke 2:46? Is it what you would expect? Why? Why not?

- In both healing episodes we observed in this chapter—the healing of the paralyzed man lowered through the roof and the healing on the Sabbath of the man with the withered hand—Jesus used questions as a part of His dialogue. How would you describe the purpose and intent of the questions in each miracle?

- If someone were to ask you about why Jesus came to earth and what His mission was, how would you reply?

- What did you observe and learn in this chapter about the power of asking questions?

- What's intimidating about the thought of asking questions like Jesus did?

CHAPTER
4

But who do you say that I am?

JESUS; MATTHEW 16:15

QUESTIONS CENTRAL TO THE MINISTRY OF JESUS

IN OUR JOURNEY to explore the art of listening and the power of asking questions, demonstrated perfectly by our Savior, Jesus Christ, we come to a pivotal moment in the ministry of Jesus, which is recorded in the Gospel of Matthew. This passage reveals the importance of attentive listening and showcases the impact of thoughtful and strategic questions. Let's take a look:

> Now when Jesus came into the district of Caesarea Philippi, He asked His disciples, "Who do people say that the Son of Man is?" And they said, "Some say John the Baptist, others say Elijah, and others Jeremiah or one of the prophets." He said to them, "But who do you say that I am?" Simon Peter replied, "You are the Christ, the Son of the living God." (MATTHEW 16:13-16)

Imagine the scene: Jesus and His disciples are in the region of Caesarea Philippi, north of Galilee, outside the land of Israel. It's a place known for its diverse religious beliefs. Here, Jesus engages His disciples in an insightful conversation, masterfully using strategic questions. "Who do people say that the Son of Man is?" This is not a casual question. He wants His disciples to listen to the opinions and beliefs circulating around them and come to grips with what He has told them and showed them.

The disciples respond by reporting what they have heard from the people. They acknowledge the popular opinions. Some think Jesus is John the Baptist. Others believe He is Elijah. Still others see Him as a prophet. Here, we see the disciples actively listening and conveying the opinions of those they've encountered. They know the mindset of the audience they are trying to reach. Their act of listening is essential to understanding the world's viewpoints and fostering meaningful discussions.

Jesus doesn't stop there. He turns the conversation to His disciples, prompting them to answer a pivotal question about themselves: "But who do *you* say that I am?" (emphasis added). This question encourages introspection and self-reflection. The disciples have relayed what the people are saying about Jesus; now He asks them to speak for themselves and tell Him who they think He is and why they're with Him.

Simon Peter, known for his spontaneous nature, responds, "You are the Christ [the Messiah], the Son of the living God." In this moment, we witness the impact of the right question. Jesus' query is a catalyst for Peter to confess His faith. This question, framed to provoke a deeper understanding, invites Peter to express his heart and soul. It offers Peter the opportunity, by the power of the Holy Spirit, to give witness and testimony to who Jesus is. As Jesus Himself observed, the ability to make this confession came from "My Father who is in heaven" (Matthew 16:17). And not only does Jesus' question draw Peter nearer to Jesus but everyone present is drawn nearer to Him as well. They hear again that Jesus' authority is not that of an earthly king; it is holy authority that came from God Himself.

This theme surfaces repeatedly in the ministry of Jesus; it's there for our benefit: the power and potential of the questions of Jesus to call people closer to Him, to take them beyond their preconceived notions and understandings so they can grasp the identity and power of Jesus. Let's take a look at another example of this theme.

A remarkable moment recorded in Matthew demonstrates how Jesus used the art of questioning as a catalyst for human transformation.

Here is the scene:

A great multitude has been with Jesus for three days, listening to His teachings and witnessing His miracles. They are hungry, and their physical needs cannot be ignored. In this moment, Jesus shows how to address real-world problems through listening and questioning.

Then Jesus called His disciples to Him and said, "I have compassion on the crowd because they have been with Me now three days and have nothing to eat. And I am unwilling to send them away hungry, lest they faint on the way." And the disciples said to Him, "Where are we to get enough bread in such a desolate place to

feed so great a crowd?" And Jesus said to them, "How many loaves do you have?" They said, "Seven, and a few small fish." (MATTHEW 15:32-39)

Jesus, deeply moved by the crowd's physical hunger, expresses His compassion for them. He sees the spiritual hunger in their hearts and acknowledges their immediate, tangible needs. Jesus turns to His disciples and asks a question that puzzles them: "How many loaves do you have?" The question is not asked in an effort to gain information but to prompt the disciples to observe the obvious. They respond, "Seven, and a few small fish." Their answer, which acknowledges their inability to feed the multitude, is an important step in the process. By asking the question, Jesus initiates a dialogue that lets the disciples see behind the curtains so that they will be aware of what He is doing.

What follows is one of the most famous miracles in the Bible. Jesus takes the seven loaves and the few small fish, blesses them, and multiplies them to feed the entire multitude. This miracle showcases the identity of Jesus as the Son of God. The disciples and all present witness Jesus' power over nature and His ability—and His willingness—to satisfy their needs. But don't overlook the fact that He uses a question to draw the disciples into the moment. Through their participation, the disciples become instruments of divine providence and abundance—the miracle is literally distributed by their hands. And it all started with a need, a question, and His provision.

Interestingly, this is not the only time Jesus asks questions that don't seem to fit the moment, at least according to our human perspective. Again, Jesus knew the word on the street about Him. He didn't need to ask His disciples, yet He still did. He knew what His disciples thought of Him, yet He still asked. He knew the crowd was hungry, He knew they had no easy or quick means of getting food, and He (most likely) knew how much bread and fish were on the premises. He didn't need to ask, but the questions weren't for His benefit; they were for the people present and for us.

Here are two more powerful examples of Jesus asking questions for the benefit of the hearer. Both involve a question before a healing. Take a look:

> **And they came to Jericho. And as He was leaving Jericho with His disciples and a great crowd, Bartimaeus, a blind beggar, the son of Timaeus, was sitting by the roadside. And when he heard that it was Jesus of Nazareth, he began to cry out and say, "Jesus, Son of David, have mercy on me!" And many rebuked him, telling him to be silent. But he cried out all the more, "Son of David, have mercy on me!" And Jesus stopped and said, "Call him." And they called the blind man, saying to him, "Take heart. Get up; He is calling you." And throwing off his cloak, he sprang up and came to Jesus. And Jesus said to him, "What do you want Me to do for you?" And the blind man said to Him, "Rabbi, let me recover my sight." And Jesus said to him, "Go your way; your faith has made you well." And**

immediately he recovered his sight and followed Him on the way. (MARK 10:46-52, EMPHASIS ADDED)

In his cry for help, Bartimaeus exemplifies the act of reaching out and acknowledging his need for something beyond himself. The crowd surrounding Jesus attempts to silence Bartimaeus. They consider his cries to be a disturbance, an interruption to the flow of things. Yet Bartimaeus persists. He is determined to be heard, even when the world tells him to be quiet, because he sees with his heart what the others do not see with their eyes: Jesus is the promised Messiah. The drama must have been intense!

In this crucial moment, Jesus turns His attention to Bartimaeus. He asks a question that may appear simple, but its depth lies in the invitation it extends: "What do you want Me to do for you?" Jesus, fully aware of Bartimaeus's blindness, still asks the question. It's an invitation to draw near, a prompt for Bartimaeus to articulate his need and desire.

A similar approach is revealed in John 5, where Jesus asks a question that at first appears to have an obvious answer, yet its depth lies in the invitation it extends:

After this there was a feast of the Jews, and Jesus went up to Jerusalem. Now there is in Jerusalem by the Sheep Gate a pool, in Aramaic called Bethesda, which has five roofed colonnades. In these lay a multitude of invalids—blind, lame, and paralyzed. One man was there who had been an invalid for thirty-eight years. When Jesus saw

him lying there and knew that he had already been there a long time, He said to him, "Do you want to be healed?" The sick man answered Him, "Sir, I have no one to put me into the pool when the water is stirred up, and while I am going another steps down before me." Jesus said to him, "Get up, take up your bed, and walk." (JOHN 5:1-8)

The scene is set at the pool of Bethesda, a place known for its miraculous healing properties. A great multitude of people, all afflicted with various illnesses, gather around the pool, hoping to be the first to step in when the water is stirred, believing this would bring their healing. Among the crowd is a man who has been paralyzed for thirty-eight years. Because of this paralysis, he cannot make it to the water in time to be healed, and no one is there to help him get in the water. After this many years, he has likely lost hope, and his life is marked by despair and longing for healing. In this account, Jesus arrives at the pool and sees the man. The man's condition is clear, and Jesus asks if he wants to be healed.

Why would Jesus ask a question with such an obvious answer? To us, it seems unnecessary. But Jesus' question is not for gathering information; it is an invitation to the man to consider his own will and faith in Jesus to bring healing to his life. The question is strategic and impactful. Jesus draws the man closer and displays His power over affliction to all who are present.

Then, to the man's expression of desire and helplessness, Jesus says, "Get up, take up your bed, and walk."

The man is immediately healed. This miracle is not just a physical restoration; it is the transformation of a life once paralyzed by despair.

We see Jesus take this approach over and over with His disciples, with those needing healing, and with those who want to know more about who He is. We see it with those who weren't sure what to make of Him and those actively working against Him. Let's look at one example closely.

In Luke 20, we find a master class in the art of questioning. In this exchange, Jesus engages with the Jewish religious leaders, strategically and intentionally using a question that challenges their hearts and invites them to deeper reflection.

One day, as Jesus was teaching the people in the temple and preaching the gospel, the chief priests and the scribes with the elders came up and said to Him, "Tell us by what authority You do these things, or who it is that gave You this authority." He answered them, "I also will ask you a question. Now tell Me, was the baptism of John from heaven or from man?" And they discussed it with one another, saying, "If we say, 'From heaven,' He will say, 'Why did you not believe him?' But if we say, 'From man,' all the people will stone us to death, for they are convinced that John was a prophet." So they answered that they did not know where it came from. And Jesus said to them, "Neither will I tell you by what authority I do these things." (LUKE 20:1-8)

The stage is set in Jerusalem during the final days of Jesus' earthly ministry. The Jewish religious leaders, who have been increasingly critical of and threatened by His teachings, waylay Him with questions. They aim to trap Him, to catch Him by His own words and discredit His authority.

Their opening question is calculated: "Tell us by what authority You do these things, or who it is that gave You this authority." They hope to force Him to admit His authority or risk being accused of blasphemy or insurrection.

Jesus, ever the master teacher, responds not with a direct answer, but with a counterquestion: "I also will ask you a question," He says. "Now tell Me, was the baptism of John from heaven or from man?" Here Jesus redirects the focus from His authority to the intentions of the religious leaders.

They are caught off guard by this and find themselves in a dilemma. They dare not answer honestly because it could expose their hypocrisy and reveal their true motivations. Their conflict becomes apparent as they weigh the consequences of their response. Eventually, they realize anything they say will get them in trouble with other religious leaders or the people they are responsible for.

It's important to note that Jesus isn't being evasive or belligerent. Rather, He is again employing the art of asking questions to teach about His authority as God the Son. These questions invite the Jewish leadership to reflect and reconsider their understanding.

Asking thought-provoking and reflective questions was central to Jesus' ministry. Better than anyone who ever walked on earth, He knew the human mind and the questions that would be the best means and mechanism to initiate self-reflection and work transformation in His people.

Before we transition to what this all means for us, there's one more consideration of Jesus' ministry I'd like to make. It's my favorite question-laced dialogue Jesus gave in the Bible, and it's worth a deep dive.

QUESTIONS FOR CONVERSATION AND REFLECTION

- How do you think the disciples felt when Jesus asked, "Who do you say that I am?"

- Would you describe that question as basic or complex? Why?

- If Jesus were to ask you, "Who do you say that I am?" how would you respond?

- What did the disciples learn from being included in the miracle of the feeding of the five thousand?

- What do you make of Jesus asking questions with seemingly obvious answers: "What do you want Me to do for you?" and "Do you want to be healed?" Why would Jesus ask these questions?

- In the example from Luke 20, how does the question Jesus asks diffuse the tension?

CHAPTER
5

What is this conversation that you are holding with each other as you walk?

JESUS; LUKE 24:17

THE BEST FOR LAST

I PRAY THAT, as you continue to read this book, it will be a blessing for you and that you will see the heart of our Savior, Jesus Christ, for His people and how that heart is reflected in His approach to us. In this chapter, I've saved what I consider to be the best example for last!

In our exploration of the significance of listening and asking questions, we turn to one of the most beautiful stories in the Gospels, which is found in Luke 24:13–35. The journey to Emmaus is a remarkable narrative that demonstrates how Jesus, in this postresurrection appearance, engaged with His disciples by simply walking alongside them, listening, and asking questions. As we unpack it, be on the lookout for the unique approach Jesus took.

That very day two of them were going to a village named Emmaus, about seven miles from Jerusalem, and they were talking with each other about all these things that had happened. While they were talking and discussing together, Jesus Himself drew near and went with them. But their eyes were kept from recognizing Him. And He said to them, "What is this conversation that you

are holding with each other as you walk?" And they stood still, looking sad. Then one of them, named Cleopas, answered Him, "Are You the only visitor to Jerusalem who does not know the things that have happened there in these days?" And He said to them, "What things?" And they said to Him, "Concerning Jesus of Nazareth, a man who was a prophet mighty in deed and word before God and all the people, and how our chief priests and rulers delivered Him up to be condemned to death, and crucified Him. But we had hoped that He was the one to redeem Israel. Yes, and besides all this, it is now the third day since these things happened. Moreover, some women of our company amazed us. They were at the tomb early in the morning, and when they did not find His body, they came back saying that they had even seen a vision of angels, who said that He was alive. Some of those who were with us went to the tomb and found it just as the women had said, but Him they did not see." And He said to them, "O foolish ones, and slow of heart to believe all that the prophets have spoken! Was it not necessary that the Christ should suffer these things and enter into His glory?" And beginning with Moses and all the Prophets, He interpreted to them in all the Scriptures the things concerning Himself.

So they drew near to the village to which they were going. He acted as if He were going farther, but they urged Him strongly, saying, "Stay with us, for it is toward evening and the day is now far spent." So He went in to stay with them. When He was at table with them, He took the bread and blessed and broke it and gave it to them. And their eyes were opened, and they recognized Him. And He vanished from their sight. They said to each other, "Did not our hearts burn within us while He talked to us on the road, while He opened to us the Scriptures?" And they rose that same hour and returned to Jerusalem. And they found the eleven and those who were with them gathered together, saying, "The Lord has risen indeed, and has appeared to Simon!" Then they told what had happened on the road, and how He was known to them in the breaking of the bread. (LUKE 24:13–35)

The account begins with two disciples walking on the road to Emmaus on the day of Jesus' resurrection and talking about "all these things that had happened." Only one of them is named (Cleopas), but Luke identifies them as disciples, so while not part of the Twelve, they were likely among the seventy-two Jesus called to be missionaries (see Luke 10:1–20). These men would be well aware of His teachings, His miracles, His death, and His empty tomb, which was discovered that morning.

As we see in verse 17, they are sad. They likely had hopes for a future with Jesus that included peace and freedom from Roman rule, but on Good Friday, those expectations were destroyed. So here they are dejected, mourning, without hope, and probably returning home to start a new life or pick up the life they abandoned when they followed Jesus into ministry.

One of my family's favorite summer vacation spots is a large water park in central Wisconsin. I love seeing my kids have fun and enjoy time with their cousins. However, I am not a big fan of heights, so I generally take a pass on tall waterslides. One time, however, I thought I had enough courage to try one.

As I was walking up the many flights of stairs, I started to chicken out. "I don't think I can do this. I'm going back," I said to my brother-in-law.

He replied, "That's going to be a tough walk down."

Confused, I asked, "What do you mean?"

His reply spoke truth: "You'll have to pass everyone coming up the stairs, and they'll know you bailed."

I thought about it for a second, looked at the stairs ahead of me, and bailed! I made that difficult walk with my head held down in shame and didn't look up. That's how I imagine the disciples here: walking, mourning, questioning, full of shame and uncertainty—and with their heads down.

Although the risen Christ is with them on the journey, He doesn't make a grand entrance. We don't know why the disciples are "kept from recognizing Him." We do know, however, that as they walk, Jesus listens to their conversation. He hears their sorrow, confusion, and frustration as they recount the events of their Teacher's death and resurrection. In this act of listening, Jesus shows us the benefit of being present and attentive to others' concerns and emotions.

Although Jesus knows the whole story (it's His story!), He asks, "What is this conversation that you are holding with each other as you walk?" His question prompts them to share their feelings and thoughts. This interaction reveals a fundamental aspect of Jesus' character: He values the voices and experiences of His followers. He cares enough to hear them, to listen to them, to ensure they are heard. That is why prayer is such a beautiful gift—it is the Lord actually hearing us!

As they walk, Jesus unfolds the Scriptures and explains how they point to Him. He reveals the grand narrative of God's plan of salvation. It is through this dialogue and exposition of Old Testament prophecy that their hearts begin to burn with understanding and faith.

The climactic moment comes when Jesus joins them for a meal. As He takes the bread, blesses it, and breaks it, their eyes are opened, and they recognize Him. In that instant, they realize that Jesus had been with them all along.

Reflect with me for a moment on how perfectly this episode fits in with the theme of this book. Here we see Jesus displaying patience, kindness, and compassion with His disciples. We might expect a grand entrance, a Palm Sunday–style, postresurrection-and-conquering-death-and-the-grave sort of procession. (That's what I would do!) Instead, He comes listening, walking alongside them, and asking questions. He does it all with the same goal He always has: "to seek and to save the lost" (Luke 19:10), to draw them closer to Himself, to point out the way to salvation.

Consider also how perfectly this bookends with how we first see Jesus as a twelve-year-old boy. That is in Luke 2, where Jesus is among the Jewish leadership "sitting among the teachers, listening to them and asking them questions" (v. 46). Here, near the end of Jesus' time on earth, He is walking alongside His people, listening to them and asking them questions! That's why I love this scene!

The congregation I serve is blessed to be part of the Comfort Dog Ministry through Lutheran Church Charities. Comfort Dog Tobias is placed with us as a deployed missionary, and boy is he popular! People love Tobias! For many years now, I've seen how dynamic and fruitful Comfort Dog Ministry truly is. Whether Tobias is visiting local elementary schools, nursing homes, or mental health facilities as a part of his everyday ministry, or if he's deployed after a weather disaster or an act of violence, the approach of the handlers is the same. It's an approach centered on and rooted in being present with people, asking good questions, and listening. I recently spoke with Jenni Hoffmeyer, Tobias's handler, about visiting with people at funerals, for example. Here's what she said:

> When Jesus asked someone a question, He already knew the answer. We don't have that same knowledge. When I enter a situation, questions help me understand the person in front of me. Listening to their responses provides me with a window into their perspective, rather than my own. People at funerals can be sad because they

knew the person who died or because this death reminds them of somebody else's passing. Or they may be in the midst of a health crisis, and the funeral reminds them of their own mortality. Questions focus the lens into someone's view of life events.

On the road to Emmaus, we witness a profound example of how Jesus Christ Himself employed the art of listening and asking questions and walking alongside people to guide them toward understanding and discovering Him. It's an approach to ministry modeled exceptionally well by Comfort Dog Ministry handlers like Jenni, and it's one we would do well to follow too. In a few chapters, we'll begin to see what that looks like. But first, after taking an in-depth look at these examples of Jesus, let's put them all together and draw some conclusions about the why behind Jesus' approach.

QUESTIONS FOR
CONVERSATION AND REFLECTION

- What would you expect Jesus to do after He rose from the dead? What kind of entrance would you expect Him to make?

- What part of the conversation that Jesus had with His disciples on the road to Emmaus is most interesting or surprising to you?

- Why do you think Jesus chose to take this approach with the disciples on the road to Emmaus?

- How would you describe the approach twelve-year-old Jesus took in the temple and the similar approach He took on the road to Emmaus?

- What can we learn from the account of the road to Emmaus?

- What strikes you about the approach of Comfort Dog Ministry?

- What can we learn from this approach to human interaction?

CHAPTER
6

And why are you
anxious about clothing?

JESUS; MATTHEW 6:28

THE "WHY" BEHIND IT ALL

AS A TWELVE-YEAR-OLD boy, throughout His ministry on earth, and with His disciples on the road to Emmaus, Jesus took the same approach in conversation with people. His goal is clear, as we discussed, in Luke 19:10: "For the Son of Man came to seek and to save the lost." Jesus came to draw all people to Himself so that we might know the depths and full extent of His love for us, shown most clearly in His suffering, death, and victory over the grave to forgive our sins and earn eternal life for us. That's why it's worthwhile to explore the why of the strategy and approach Jesus took. Said a different way, of all the methods Jesus could have used, why did He so often choose to listen and then ask questions?

TOP 10 WAYS AND REASONS JESUS TOOK THIS UNIQUE APPROACH

1. Transformational Teaching: Unlike many teachers of His time who primarily imparted knowledge through lecture and monologue, Jesus used questions to engage His listeners actively in the learning process. His conversations aimed not just to inform but also to challenge people's thinking, beliefs, and behaviors.

Think about the last time you heard an extended lecture. It's hard to stay dialed in to all the presenter is conveying if all he or she is doing is talking at you. After a while, it feels like your personal listening bucket is full and there is no more room. Questions, however, move the listener from merely receiving information to actively transforming thoughts, beliefs, and actions. Monologues impart knowledge; questions spur reflection and transformation.

Consider Jesus' statement in Luke 6:46: "Why do you call Me 'Lord, Lord,' and not do what I tell you?" This question spurred reflection. The audience, His disciples, heard His question and may have thought, "I do call You Lord, and I *do* want to do what You say!" It's a question that causes its hearers to consider their thoughts, beliefs, and actions.

2. Revealing Truth through Parables: Jesus frequently used parables, which I've heard defined as "earthly stories with heavenly meanings." It is through parables that Jesus taught truths about the kingdom of God, how things work in God's economy, and how His followers are to live among others. These are stories with disguised meanings that reveal and teach profound spiritual truths. Master-storyteller Jesus knew that one of the most effective ways to communicate truth was through stories that combine familiar situations and settings with important lessons.

Depending on how you count them, Jesus told as many as fifty parables. Many times, questions accompanied them.

Questions within parables encouraged listeners to draw conclusions and uncover deeper insights for themselves, promoting active participation and understanding. Take, for example, the parable of the Good Samaritan, which Jesus concludes with this question: "Which of these three, do you think, proved to be a neighbor to the man who fell among the robbers?" (Luke 10:36). So, after a dynamic and dramatic parable, Jesus guides His listeners from merely hearing it to processing the truth behind it: that the Good Samaritan is like Jesus, who has compassion on us and heals us, even though we are His enemy.

3. Personal Engagement: Jesus' questions were deeply personal and individualized. He addressed people's unique circumstances, needs, and backgrounds, showing that He saw and cared for each person.

Think back to the example I used to launch this book—the story of me in my role as a fire department chaplain responding to a family after the death of their grandmother and mother. I made false assumptions that hindered my ability to provide care, but then I transitioned to asking questions that were personal and individual, thus enabling me to serve the family better. Or consider the example provided in the preceding chapter by Comfort Dog Tobias's handler, Jenni Hoffmeyer, who asks personal and individual questions to help get to the source of the hurt so she can better provide comfort. Jesus, in His ministry, did the same and did it perfectly.

A great example of this is in John 21. After His resurrection, Jesus is with His disciples. One of those disciples is Peter, who had done what he said he would never do: deny knowing Jesus. Three times, in fact, Peter did what he said he would never do. Now, postresurrection, they are all back together. How is Jesus going to treat Peter? He begins with a question: "Simon, son of John, do you love Me more than these?" (v. 15). Think about it. The process to redeem and reinstate Peter begins with a question. Me? I'd begin with, "I can't believe you did that to me!" Not Jesus. It's a deeply personal and individual question, and it begins the journey to healing and restoration.

4. Probing the Heart: Many of Jesus' questions focused on matters of the heart, exposing motivations and attitudes. He wasn't content with superficial obedience; He sought genuine repentance from the inside out. He knew that questions were the best way to get His people to recognize their sin, comprehend their need for a Savior, and find forgiveness and peace in Him.

Consider Matthew 6, an extended teaching called the Sermon on the Mount, regarding worry and anxiety and other matters of the heart. Included in this teaching is a question: "And why are you anxious about clothing?" (v. 28). It's Jesus' way of asking what's underneath our worry and concern. Rather than lecturing about God's history of providence and provision for His people and scolding them for moments when they don't trust in Him, He uses the power of a question to help them see that all they are looking for is found only in Him. And when He asks it like that, "Why are you anxious about clothing?" it really puts their lack of faith into perspective. It leads a follower of Jesus to say, "You're right, Jesus. I am afraid. But our heavenly Father provides what I truly need. Help me to trust Him, stop worrying, and pray to Him instead."

5. Challenging Hypocrisy: Jesus' questions often challenged the hypocrisy of religious leaders and those who claimed righteousness but lacked genuine faith. His questions exposed the gap between their outward appearances of piety and inner reality of faithlessness. The questions of Jesus weren't just for His disciples; they were also for those who challenged Him and rejected Him. And He used questions to expose them as hypocrites. Take, for example, the story of the crippled woman healed on the Sabbath in Luke 13. After Jesus heals her in the synagogue, here's what happens next:

> **But the ruler of the synagogue, indignant because Jesus had healed on the Sabbath, said to the people, "There are six days in which work ought to be done. Come on those days and be healed, and not on the Sabbath day." Then the Lord answered him, "You hypocrites!** *Does not each of you on the Sabbath untie his ox or his donkey from the manger and lead it away to water it? And ought not this woman, a daughter of Abraham whom Satan bound for eighteen years, be loosed from this bond on the Sabbath day?"* **As He said these things, all His adversaries were put to shame, and all the people rejoiced at all the glorious things that were done by Him.** (LUKE 13:14-17, EMPHASIS ADDED).

In a beautiful, powerful way, Jesus uses questions to expose their hypocrisy and elevate the values of love and compassion. These questions spur reflection and self-examination for the Jewish leadership, and also for everyone in the audience.

6. Creating Memorable Moments: Jesus' questions created memorable interactions that left a lasting impact on His listeners. The questions He asked were thought-provoking, making His teachings more memorable and more likely to be shared and discussed after His ministry on earth was accomplished. His questions often created powerful, dramatic scenes, and while they were sometimes complex, other times, they were quite simple and straightforward:

As Jesus went, the people pressed around Him. And there was a woman who had had a discharge of blood for twelve years, and though she had spent all her living on physicians, she could not be healed by anyone. She came up behind Him and touched the fringe of His garment, and immediately her discharge of blood ceased. And Jesus said, *"Who was it that touched Me?"* When all denied it, Peter said, "Master, the crowds surround You and are pressing in on You!" But Jesus said, "Someone touched Me, for I perceive that power has gone out from Me." And when the woman saw that she was not hidden, she came trembling, and falling down before Him declared in the presence of

all the people why she had touched Him, and how she had been immediately healed. And He said to her, "Daughter, your faith has made you well; go in peace." (LUKE 8:42-48, EMPHASIS ADDED)

What's ironic about Jesus asking "Who was it that touched Me?" is that He is the omniscient Son of God, so of course He knows who touched Him! But He uses the question to draw the healed woman back into the scene, where she falls down in worship before Him.

7. Empowering through Learning: Jesus used questions to empower His disciples and followers to think critically and teach them about the kingdom of God. By challenging them to wrestle with important questions, He helped them develop a deeper understanding of spiritual truths. Jesus is a master teacher, after all, and knows that questions empower learners to, by the power of the Holy Spirit, be led to new realities about who He is.

I love when Jesus does this in Luke 14. It's a conversation with His disciples about what it looks like to follow Him. He wants them to give full consideration about what it's going to mean for them and uses questions to help them learn.

Whoever does not bear his own cross and come after Me cannot be My disciple. *For which of you, desiring to build a tower, does not first sit down and count the cost, whether he has enough to complete it?* Otherwise, when he has laid a foundation and is not able to finish, all who see it

begin to mock him, saying, "This man began to build and was not able to finish." *Or what king, going out to encounter another king in war, will not sit down first and deliberate whether he is able with ten thousand to meet him who comes against him with twenty thousand?* And if not, while the other is yet a great way off, he sends a delegation and asks for terms of peace. So therefore, any one of you who does not renounce all that he has cannot be My disciple. (LUKE 14:27-33, EMPHASIS ADDED)

Rather than saying, "Consider the ramifications of following Me," Jesus uses questions that spark self-examination and self-reflection. He speaks in terms His followers readily understand to cause them to consider what life as His disciple will be like.

8. Cultivating Relationship: Jesus' questions opened the door for meaningful conversations in order to connect with people on a personal level, demonstrating care and interest in their lives. This is who Jesus was during His ministry on earth. It was core to His identity as Redeemer, who reconciled sinful mankind with the Lord God.

Consider the dramatic exchange that takes place in John 6:

After this many of His disciples turned back and no longer walked with Him. So Jesus said to the twelve, *"Do you want to go away as well?"* Simon Peter answered Him, "Lord, to whom shall we go? You have the words of eternal life, and we have

believed, and have come to know, that You are the Holy One of God." (JOHN 6:66-69, EMPHASIS ADDED)

Following Jesus was difficult and countercultural, and some chose to turn back and no longer walk with Him. To get the disciples to commit to their relationship with Him and to confess who He is, Jesus puts them on the spot: "Do you want to go away as well?" And here, Peter, empowered by the Holy Spirit, speaks directly to the truth of who Jesus is. It's a beautiful moment spurred on by a straightforward question.

9. Pointing to Spiritual Realities: Jesus' questions directed people's attention to spiritual realities and eternal truths. Through His questions, He encouraged listeners to consider aspects beyond the physical world and temporary concerns and to instead consider eternal realities.

I love how Jesus does just this in Matthew 18. Check it out, and be on the lookout for how Jesus helps His people uncover the very heart of God:

What do you think? If a man has a hundred sheep, and one of them has gone astray, does he not leave the ninety-nine on the mountains and go in search of the one that went astray? And if he finds it, truly, I say to you, he rejoices over it more than over the ninety-nine that never went astray. So it is not the will of My Father who is in heaven that one of these little ones should perish. (MATTHEW 18:12-14)

Jesus wants His audience to grasp the Father's love for all people, that He is indeed a God who seeks and saves, and that He is the Shepherd who seeks the lost (Luke 19:10). Rather than merely saying it, Jesus uses a story with a familiar setting to illustrate for His listeners the relentless, compassionate heart of their heavenly Father.

10. Modeling Humility: Jesus engaged in dialogue and encouraged open communication. One memorable example of this is found in John 4, the exchange Jesus has with the Samaritan woman at the well. The conversation begins with a simple statement: "Give Me a drink" (John 4:7). Hot, tired, and thirsty, Jesus shows His humanity by asking for water from one who has the means to draw it. This statement is also strategic in that it is an entrance to further dialogue and leads to a complex conversation about the relationship between Jewish people and Samaritans. Because of the social and cultural differences, the woman is shocked by His statement. But it shows us that Jesus doesn't avoid the sinner. Rather, He comes face to face with her. Jesus reveals His identity as the long-promised Messiah—someone so significant that even Samaritans outside the Jewish community know who He is. He humbles Himself to meet her where she is, acknowledge her circumstances, and address her needs.

This was a powerful and transformative tool in Jesus' ministry. He challenged, inspired, transformed, and led people to a deeper understanding of God's kingdom and to recognize who He was as the Messiah, the Son of God. His questions were a reflection of both His wisdom and

His teaching style. Most of all, they served to reveal His identity to His people.

Having given helpful treatment to the role of listening and asking questions in the ministry of Jesus, the next section will explore how this approach is echoed in the Pauline Epistles and the rest of the New Testament.

QUESTIONS FOR
CONVERSATION AND REFLECTION

- What is it, in your estimation, that makes asking questions a worthwhile and successful approach for building relationships?

- Can you think of a time when you were asked a question that invited you to reconsider your position or approach?

- Can you think of a time when you asked someone a question that helped him or her reconsider his or her position or approach?

- How might asking questions help diffuse conflict or tension?

- How do questions communicate humility?

- Of the ten listed ways and reasons Jesus used to listen and ask questions, which do you find the most compelling?

CHAPTER

7

What do you want Me
to do for you?

JESUS; MATTHEW 20:32

ECHOES IN THE NEW TESTAMENT

JESUS CHRIST, THE very Son of God, came to earth to give His life as a ransom for all mankind.

> **For even the Son of Man came not to be served but to serve, and to give His life as a ransom for many.** (MARK 10:45)

It's who He is. It's why He came. In hopes of drawing all people to Himself, He intentionally and strategically took an approach of patiently walking alongside people, listening to them and asking them questions to open their ears to hear His message. As we've seen, this approach was efficacious and winsome on many levels, and the Gospels reveal this approach.

The rest of the New Testament, which includes letters to the first Christians and descriptions of what the early church was like, reinforces that this was not only what Jesus did and the approach Jesus took but also what His *followers* were to do and the approach they were to take.

Before we look at how the Christian, fueled by the Holy Spirit, is to follow the example of Jesus Christ, let's review what the New Testament says about a foundational aspect of the character of God:

I write these things to you who believe in the name of the Son of God, that you may know that you have eternal life. And this is the confidence that we have toward Him, that if we ask anything according to His will He hears us. And if we know that He hears us in whatever we ask, we know that we have the requests that we have asked of Him. (1 JOHN 5:13-15)

I fear that many of us have heard this truth so many times that it's lost meaning and power; dare I say, it's scandal. That truth I'm referring to is this—the Lord of all creation, the Creator, Redeemer, and Sustainer of all things, the One who holds all of the universe in the palm of His hand, the One who daily (second by second) ensures that the air we breathe has just the right combination of oxygen, nitrogen, carbon dioxide, and other elements so we can continue to breathe, actually humbles Himself to listen to us! What? Read that sentence again, and let it sink in. The King of the universe *listens* to you whenever you talk to Him. Now that's a scandal!

We could call it the humility of God to hear us, and that would make sense—God humbles Himself to hear us. There's another word I like to use regarding this aspect of God's character—*condescension*. Often, condescension is used in a negative sense, as though someone were speaking in a condescending tone. But a second dictionary definition from *Merriam-Webster* describes it this way: "voluntary descent from one's rank or dignity in relations with an inferior." That is an apt description of God listening to us. He is indeed voluntarily descending from His rank and dignity as Lord of all things to be in relationship with inferiors—you and me!

Think of it like this: what if you went to the driving range to hit a few golf balls, and Tiger Woods came over and listened as you provided some swing tips? Or what if you went to the local coffee house on open mic night, and Taylor Swift came to pick your brain and listen to your performance advice? That doesn't sound or feel right, does it?

Yet the Bible promises it to be true: "If we ask anything according to His will *He hears us*" (emphasis added).

So, if the Lord of all creation would deign to humble Himself, condescend to hear us, how could we not follow Jesus' example and take time to listen patiently with our brothers and sisters? Think about it this way: each time you humble yourself and listen to another person—genuinely listen—you are doing what the Lord God promises to do with you. As the apostle Paul writes, "Be imitators of me, as I am of Christ" (1 Corinthians 11:1).

And this is exactly what we have been called to do. Listening is an action, no doubt, of showing love, care, and compassion for another. But even more than that, as we'll explore in subsequent chapters, it's an attitude and a posture that places others above yourself. Philippians 2:1–5 puts it beautifully. Look for how this is an attitude, a posture:

So if there is any encouragement in Christ, any comfort from love, any participation in the Spirit, any affection and sympathy, complete my joy by being of the same mind, having the same love, being in full accord and of one mind. Do nothing from selfish ambition or conceit, but in humility count others more significant than yourselves. Let each of you look not only to his own interests, but also to the interests of others. Have this mind among yourselves, which is yours in Christ Jesus.

Two aspects of this text jump out for me. First, everything we do as Christians, a people redeemed by the blood of Jesus Christ, is rooted in what He first did for us. Since we have received everything from Christ and are in Christ, we should follow His way. Second, in response to the work of the Lord in us, we are to "count others more significant than [ourselves]" and "look not only to [our] own interests, but also to the interests of others." Jesus put our needs above His own by going to the cross for us; therefore, we should put others above ourselves. This means truly listening to them!

Building on the posture and attitude described in Philippians 2, Paul adds this thoughtful statement in 1 Corinthians 8:2: "If anyone imagines that he knows something, he does not yet know as he ought to know." What a humility-inspiring passage! Said a different way, If you think you know everything, think again! This is a helpful reminder to us. We don't know everything, and taking a posture of curiosity and growth is a great relationship-building posture (much more on this later).

Finally, two chapters later and in the same vein, Paul shares this: "Therefore let anyone who thinks that he stands take heed lest he fall" (1 Corinthians 10:12). Remember, the apostle Paul spent much of his previous life, his life preconversion, convinced that he was better than everyone. Read how he describes his former attitude in Philippians 3:4: "If anyone else thinks he has reason for confidence in the flesh, I have more." This is how he once was. Now, in Christ, he is a new creation (see 2 Corinthians 5:17). And that new creation, in Paul and in us, puts others before self. It recognizes that it doesn't know everything. It takes a posture of humility and curiosity. The new creation listens and asks good questions.

And it's who Jesus was first for us.

QUESTIONS FOR
CONVERSATION AND REFLECTION

- What's crazy, almost scandalous, about the truth that the Lord God listens to us?

- When you pray, do you think of the Lord of all creation as actually listening to you?

- How is the act of listening putting others before yourself?

- Who in your life do you find it most difficult to attentively listen to?

- How is listening to others a fulfillment of Philippians 2:1-5?

- How is listening to others a fulfillment of 1 Corinthians 8:2?

CHAPTER

8

Then you will call upon Me
and come and pray to Me,
and I will hear you.

GOD; JEREMIAH 29:12

OLD TESTAMENT ROOTS

IN OUR EXPLORATION of the importance of listening and asking questions, we turn our attention to the rich tapestry woven throughout the Bible. Malachi 3:6 speaks this truth: "For I the LORD do not change." This means that what we see in the ministry of Jesus reveals the heart of God the Father. The approach Jesus takes in the New Testament is deeply rooted in the Old Testament, revealing a God who not only deigns to hear our prayers but also encourages us to actively engage in a dialogue with Him.

The prophet Jeremiah, a poignant voice in the Old Testament, conveys a message of hope and assurance from God:

Then you will call upon Me and come and pray to Me, and I will hear you. (JEREMIAH 29:12)

This verse encapsulates the essence of a God who listens to and responds to the prayers of His people. As we observed in the previous chapter, let's never overlook or take for granted that almighty God promises to hear us when we call upon Him. And every promise He makes is a promise He keeps.

Similarly, the Psalms, a poetic masterpiece, offer a glimpse into the heartfelt expressions of the writers:

> I love the LORD, because He has heard my voice and my pleas for mercy. Because He inclined His ear to me, therefore I will call on Him as long as I live. (PSALM 116:1-2)

This psalm serves as a beautiful testimony to the intimacy of a relationship with God, who not only hears but also inclines His ear to His people, who leans down and toward us in an intimate posture. What a powerful image and a memorable visual this provides! Again, this illustrates our holy God's condescension to hear us sinful humans! It's echoed earlier in the psalter:

> In my distress I called upon the LORD; to my God I cried for help. From His temple He heard my voice, and my cry to Him reached His ears. (PSALM 18:6)

Take note that both psalms celebrate what God has done, not merely what the writer of each psalm hoped He would do. The psalms celebrate that God answers His people and fulfills His promises.

Perhaps you're aware of the painting *The Creation of Adam,* the fresco by Michelangelo that is part of the Sistine Chapel's ceiling. It's a portrait of a relaxed Adam, arm on his leg, limp, while the Creator, with angels by His side, reaches to touch the human, crossing the distance to get to His creation. Michelangelo's theology here is rooted in what we read above—that God relentlessly strains to be in relationship with us. We might take this a little further and say that while sinful, selfish humanity reclines and is often indifferent to the reality of the triune God, God is constantly wooing and pursuing us. It's who He is, and His promise to hear us and listen to us is one way He puts it into practice.

This attribute of God, then, this aspect of His character, is to be reflected by His people. The followers of God are called *followers* for a reason. We are to emulate what He first does for us. Just as the Lord God listens to us with grace and understanding, we, too, are called to extend that same attentive ear to others. We saw in the preceding chapter that the Epistles call the sanctified, Holy Spirit–filled Christian to a life of putting the needs of others before the needs of self. The Old Testament sings the same song.

In the book of Proverbs, a repository of divine wisdom, we find an exhortation to embrace the art of listening:

Let the wise hear and increase in learning, and the one who understands obtain guidance. (PROVERBS 1:5)

This verse emphasizes that wisdom is acquired through listening and learning. The call to the wise to hear suggests an active engagement with the perspectives and insights of others. The Lord listens to us, so we hear and listen to others.

Another gem from Proverbs directs our attention to the significance of understanding the depths of the human heart through attentive listening:

The purpose in a man's heart is like deep water, but a man of understanding will draw it out. (PROVERBS 20:5)

This verse highlights the profound nature of human thoughts and emotions and the role of a listener in drawing out those depths through focused listening and asking thoughtful questions. Again, as the Lord is patient in hearing us, we exercise patience in hearing the needs, experiences, and hurts of others.

We also see this beautifully in many Old Testament narratives. One of my favorites is found in 2 Samuel. It's the story of King David inquiring if anyone from Jonathan's family is still alive so he may show gratitude for all Jonathan did for him:

And David said, "Is there still anyone left of the house of Saul, that I may show him kindness for Jonathan's sake?" (2 SAMUEL 9:1)

This leads David to Mephibosheth (say that five times fast!), a son of Jonathan who could not walk. Ultimately, because of David's question, Mephibosheth is given a place at David's table for all the days of his life.

And it all started with asking a really good question.

Sitting, listening, walking alongside, and asking questions were practiced so perfectly by our Lord and Savior, Jesus Christ. It was His rhythm and strategy of ministry as He relentlessly pursued personal engagement with people. And it reflected the heart of God the Father for all of humanity. This makes sense, after all, as "in Him the whole fullness of deity dwells bodily" (Colossians 2:9), meaning all the fullness of God dwells in Christ Jesus. If we want to know what God is like—His attributes—we look to Jesus. And the Old and New Testaments are in alignment in how they speak of our Lord and His compassion for His people. It's the approach He takes, and it's the approach you and I are called to seek to emulate. Now, let's take a deep dive into how this looks!

QUESTIONS FOR
CONVERSATION AND REFLECTION

- Based on what we've learned so far, how would you describe the heart of God for all people?

- How does the Lord God listening to us reflect His heart for all people?

- When have you felt heard by God?

- Is there something in your life that you want God to hear right now?

- How would you summarize what the Bible says about listening to others?

- In what ways is a person's heart "like a deep water," needing to be drawn out?

PART III

The Attitude and Posture of a Listener

CHAPTER
9

An intelligent heart acquires knowledge, and the ear of the wise seeks knowledge.

SOLOMON; PROVERBS 18:15

LIVING OCI

I LOVE WHAT we've covered so far, and I pray it's been a blessing to you. And let me tell you, I love where we're heading next! It's time to get hyper-practical. It's my vision that by the end of this book, you'll be equipped with a fresh new mindset and approach to conversations and relationships. I also hope it is a blessing to others and greatly enriches your life as well!

So far we've seen how the Lord Jesus Christ, in His earthly ministry, took an approach that was unique at that time and in that place. Rather than going village to village, telling people what to do, He intentionally and strategically used the art of asking open-ended questions to build and strengthen relationships and help people experience life transformation. The Gospel accounts record for us that Jesus asked more than three hundred questions (wow!) and used them to successfully reveal His identity and help others see how life-changing it was to be His disciple. In addition, this approach is not only a New Testament approach; we see that our God hears and listens to His people throughout the Bible. And it doesn't end there.

Hours before He is to be arrested and crucified, Jesus spends time with His disciples. It's called the Upper Room

Discourse, and it spans John 13–17. In this account, we see that Jesus knows full well His crucifixion awaits, and He desires to impart this knowledge to His closest disciples. It's almost like a last will and testament. A centerpiece, foundational element to this discourse is found early in the account:

Love one another: just as I have loved you, you also are to love one another. (JOHN 13:34)

As He loves us, so we are to love one another. Said another way, Jesus' love for us is not only exactly what we need from Him—grace, forgiveness, new life, and more—it also demonstrates how we are to interact with one another. The posture and attitude He takes with us is the posture and attitude we take in our personal relationships and interactions with others. "Just as I have loved you, you also are to love one another."

But how? What does this look like? The remainder of this book will provide you with attitudes and practices designed to help you do for others what the Lord first did for you.

Let's start with a bit of a reality check. I'm sorry to tell you, but you are probably not as good of a listener as you think you are. Let me explain.

From my experience, it strikes me that many people think they are good listeners. For example, if you had a room full of thirty people, and you asked how many consider themselves to be above-average listeners, I think many hands would go in the air. But if you asked that same group to evaluate the listening skills of others, I think they would say many people are below-average listeners. We think we're good at something that others say we're not so good at.

Bottom line: we overestimate our ability to listen well. There are many factors at play here. First, we underestimate or misread our own body language.

For example, we might believe that we give the impression that we're listening, but our body language tells a different story. Research from a number of studies indicates that as much as 93 percent of what you communicate is nonverbal![5] So while you might be thinking, *I'm not talking, so that means I'm listening*, your nonverbals are telling an entirely different story. You might be fidgeting, looking around, or even glancing at your phone; your facial expressions, body posture, breathing, and a host of other cues communicate if you are listening. This is what makes people think that others are not good listeners. And to some degree, that includes you!

Many years ago, my wife and I attended a local fundraising event. The room was full of people who served in elected office in one way or another. Not to slam on politicians, but who do you speculate the room was filled with—better talkers or better listeners? To this day, I remember one exchange in particular. Now, there were more well-known people in the room than me, but rather than making me think that I was worth conversing with, the elected official I was talking with constantly looked around the room. At one point, he even craned his neck to look around me to see if there was someone more important to talk with! I felt like saying, "I'll let you go so you can talk to people you think are more important." I've heard it said that you'll forget what people say to you, but you'll never forget how they made you feel. Years later, I have not forgotten how that person made me feel.

However, something good came out of that conversation. That night, I made a commitment to never make anyone else feel like that. People we talk with deserve our full energy and attention. As a parish pastor, Sunday mornings are busy for me. There's lots to think about, lots to do, and lots of people to talk with. But after that night, I took a different approach to my conversations before and after worship services. I made a commitment to seek to be fully present and engaged with whomever I was speaking with. Admittedly, before that fundraiser, I sometimes did the same thing at my church that the politician did to me. I would be talking with someone while also scanning the lobby and looking for guests or someone returning to church after a time away. My nonverbals communicated that others were more important than the person I was talking with! I made people in my church feel like I felt at that fundraiser. Lord, have mercy on me. And to the people of the church I serve, thank you for your grace to me. Now, by God's grace, I seek to do better.

I encourage you to take a growth mindset as you work through the remainder of this book. The reality is that listening is a growth area for all of us. Yet the good news is that there are many ways to get better at this, and doing so will strengthen your existing relationships and help you build new ones!

As we launch this section, permit me to share a foundational, guiding principle that will frame the remainder of this book. This is what makes this book unique amidst all the other voices, books, and resources that talk about improving listening skills. My main argument is this: *listening is less a series of skills to master and more a mindset, attitude, and posture.* This is rooted in what you read earlier—that hearing and listening is the mindset, attitude, and posture the Lord takes with us. Following His example is what we do for and with others. In addition, you can learn the skills, but if your heart isn't in it, the skills will fade because they aren't rooted in a specific mindset and attitude. Said in a different way, you can only fake it for so long! So in the remainder of this chapter, I outline the best way to think about what this looks like in everyday life.

I call it Living OCI.

OCI stands for Open, Curious, and Inquisitive. I like that acronym because it sounds a lot to me like CSI, the popular television series with many spin-offs. At the heart of CSI is the quest to solve crimes by following clues and being observant, perceptive, and attentive. CSI detectives must be fully present and discerning if they want to solve the crime.

In the same way, you and I, as listeners, build, rebuild, and strengthen relationships by being present, discerning, observant, perceptive, and attentive as we interact with others. That's a mouthful, I know, so I've shortened it to OCI because it's memorable and reminds me of specific things I can do while I'm listening. Let's briefly unpack each word and then take each one a bit further.

Open means that primarily, you take a posture of openness in your interactions and conversations. You are open to where the conversation may lead, open to learning something new, or open to learning more about the person with whom you are conversing. You haven't made up your mind or prejudged the other person because you celebrate that people grow and change. You are open to what the Lord, through the person and work of the Holy Spirit, might do in any given conversation. Being open means that you have not made up your mind about that person or have not taken a certain position.

Curious means that you genuinely want to know more about the other person. You are intrigued by his or her story, and you hope to understand the person's background, listening to what is going on in his or her life now and what hopes there are for the future. By being curious, you seek to serve the other person by getting to know more about him or her and because (side benefit) you, too, might grow in knowledge or understanding. Being curious means you genuinely wonder why the other person thinks or acts the way he or she does or, even better, you are eager to discover what you can learn from the other person.

Inquisitive describes the approach you take: you ask questions. Because you are open and curious, and want to learn more, and because you know the power and potential of asking questions, you take an inquisitive approach. You know from seeing how Jesus practiced this in the New Testament that asking questions spurs reflection, leads to deeper understanding, and may result in personal transformation. Good questions are truly a relationship life hack. Being inquisitive means that you declare yourself to be someone who wants to learn more and who cares about others.

That's our baseline. Now let's unpack each of these behaviors and why Living OCI is so powerful and effective.

In the intricate dance of human communication, the virtues of openness, curiosity, and inquisitiveness serve as guiding lights. Together, these qualities create a symphony of engagement that enriches relationships, fosters learning, and brings about transformative insights.

Openness is a virtue that beckons us to embrace change, acknowledging that growth often emerges from the willingness to step outside our preconceived notions and comfort zones. As we consider the significance of being open in the context of listening and questioning, we recognize that a closed mind can be a barrier to understanding, hindering the potential for transformative conversations.

Openness begins with vulnerability, the courage to expose oneself to new ideas and perspectives. In the realm of listening, being open means welcoming differing and diverse viewpoints and refraining from immediate judgment. It's an invitation to let go of preconceived notions and biases, creating an environment where meaningful dialogue can flourish. It's as simple as saying, "I'm open to learning from this person."

Openness is intricately connected to empathy, the ability to understand and share the feelings of others. In the act of listening, an open heart enables us to not only hear words but also to grasp the emotions and intentions behind them. Empathy fosters connection, breaking down walls that may impede genuine communication. Think about it: If you are closed-minded or prejudging, it's very difficult to practice empathy.

Consider a scenario where two individuals, each entrenched in their beliefs, engage in a conversation. The one who is open to change is more likely to listen with the intent to understand and to consider alternative perspectives. This models for the other, inspires the other, and reduces the tension. Openness thus becomes the catalyst for growth and mutual understanding.

Curiosity is a relentless desire for understanding, an insatiable appetite to get to the bottom of why people think the way they do. It propels us to explore the nuances of diverse perspectives and to unravel the intricacies of human thought. In the context of listening and questioning, curiosity becomes a driving force that propels us beyond the surface into the depths of comprehension.

Curiosity involves active engagement, a mental and emotional investment in the exchange of ideas. It sparks a genuine interest in the stories, experiences, histories, and beliefs that shape individuals. By delving into the motivations behind people's thoughts and actions, curiosity transforms listening from a passive activity into an enriching journey of discovery.

Imagine two colleagues engaged in a conversation about a project. The curious individual, eager to understand the rationale behind the other's approach, asks probing questions that go beyond the surface. This curiosity not only enhances their mutual understanding but it also fosters a collaborative atmosphere where diverse perspectives are valued. More times than not, the curious colleague will model for and inspire the other to do the same!

Finally, inquisitiveness is the art of asking thoughtful questions that aid in discovery. It goes beyond simple inquiry; it involves crafting questions that prompt reflection, stimulate conversation, and lead to meaningful insights. In the realm of listening and questioning, inquisitiveness becomes the key that unlocks the doors to deeper understanding. It's a practice, sure, but it's rooted in a mindset, attitude, and posture.

Effective questioning is an art and a science. It involves framing questions that invite individuals to share their thoughts, explore their feelings, and articulate their perspectives. The skill of asking good questions lies in the ability to elicit meaningful responses, guiding the conversation toward discovery and mutual comprehension.

Consider a classroom setting where a teacher employs inquisitiveness to engage students in a discussion. By asking open-ended questions that encourage critical thinking, the teacher not only assesses the students' understanding but also stimulates curiosity and a thirst for knowledge. Inquisitiveness, in this context, becomes a catalyst for discovery and learning.

I have seen this in practice as I teach confirmation class to the sixth through eighth graders at my church. As much as I want to simply impart knowledge and doctrine to them through direct instruction (that is, I speak, you listen), this is rarely the most successful and efficacious approach. Instead, when I pose a question or a problem and let the students wrestle with it, class conversation explodes like fireworks! Hands fly in the air, seeking to make sense and add to the conversation!

As we weave openness, curiosity, and inquisitiveness together, a symphony of engagement emerges—a harmonious dance that transforms conversations into vibrant exchanges of ideas, perspectives, and insights. This interplay creates an environment where listening is not a passive activity but an active, participatory journey toward understanding. It makes conversations and interactions really fun!

In personal relationships, the symphony of openness, curiosity, and inquisitiveness deepens connections. When partners are open to change, curious about each other's inner worlds, and inquisitive in their conversations, they cultivate a space where mutual growth and understanding flourish. This symphony becomes the foundation for resilient, thriving relationships.

In educational settings, the symphony of engagement fosters learning environments where students and teachers alike are open to new ideas, curious about diverse perspectives, and inquisitive in their pursuit of knowledge. The classroom becomes a dynamic space where inquiry, exploration, and discovery are celebrated. I described this in my example from confirmation class above, but it's not confined to the classroom. It could also take place at the dinner table, in the boardroom, at the church meeting, and so many more places.

The transformative power of this symphony extends beyond individual interactions. In the workplace, congregation, or community group, an organizational culture that embraces openness, curiosity, and inquisitiveness becomes a breeding ground for innovation, collaboration, and adaptability. These virtues act as catalysts for organizational growth and success. Rather than leading to a fear of change or the future, it instead leads to excitement to experience it together.

Yet let's be real. While the virtues of openness, curiosity, and inquisitiveness bring about profound rewards, they are not without challenges. Overcoming the fear of vulnerability, resisting the temptation to judge prematurely, and cultivating the discipline of active listening require intentional effort. However, the rewards far outweigh the challenges.

The reward of embracing this symphony lies in the depth of the connection it cultivates—connection to oneself, to others, and to the wealth of perspectives that surround us. Openness, curiosity, and inquisitiveness become the bridges that span the gaps between individuals, fostering a tapestry of shared understanding and leading to healthier relationships and organizations.

Finally, Living OCI, led by the Holy Spirit, is living out who the Lord has called us to be. As He is so patient, loving, and forgiving of us, we seek to take the same posture toward others.

And one more thing: it even makes the office holiday party or political fundraising event just a bit more interesting and palatable—imagine that!

QUESTIONS FOR
CONVERSATION AND REFLECTION

● Why do you suspect we are not as good at listening as we think we are?

● How and when are you a good and effective listener? How and when are you not a good and effective listener?

● Would the people around you (family, friends, coworkers) describe you as a good listener?

● What does the following statement mean to you? "Listening is less a series of skills to master and way more a mindset, attitude, and posture."

● How can you practice being open in conversations and relationships?

● What is challenging about being open in conversations and relationships?

● How can you practice being curious in conversations and relationships?

● What is challenging about being curious in conversations and relationships?

🗨 How can you practice being inquisitive in conversations and relationships?

🗨 What is challenging about being inquisitive in conversations and relationships?

CHAPTER
10

Everyone is interesting if
you ask the right questions.

ANONYMOUS

GIVE IT SOME THOUGHT

IN THE PREVIOUS chapter, we explored how effective listening is less a series of skills to master and way more a mindset, attitude, and posture. I introduced what I call Living OCI—letting openness, curiosity, and inquisitiveness be our guide. Now it's time to get specific.

While it's tempting to jump right into the conversations and what they sound and feel like, in this chapter, we will explore an underrated and surprisingly effective element that can transform those conversations. This element, one I rarely hear advocated for, has the potential to make your relationships much more meaningful. Ready for it?

It's preparation. I believe that giving the upcoming conversation some thought and doing some planning has the potential to make a mundane conversation life-giving and memorable. Let me explain.

In the intricate dance of communication, the significance of thoughtful planning cannot be overstated. Whether it's a one-on-one conversation or a meeting with multiple participants, having a well-crafted plan can transform the dynamics, turning ordinary interactions into opportunities for understanding and connection. I argue that making a plan for conversations, focusing on the importance of knowing what you want to learn, and crafting thoughtful questions can be a difference-maker. No doubt, premeditated thoughtfulness can elevate the quality of our dialogues.

The foundation of a successful conversation lies in the clarity of objectives. Before entering into any dialogue, take time to identify what you want to achieve. Are you seeking to understand a person's perspective to aid in conflict resolution, gather information to facilitate a service project, or make a decision collaboratively to achieve an organizational goal? In ministry and mission settings in particular, keeping objectives centered on the work God has called us to do—our vocations—sets the stage for focused and purposeful conversations.

Consider a scenario where you're having a conversation with a colleague about his or her career goals. Your objective might be to understand your colleague's aspirations, identify potential areas for growth within the organization, and explore opportunities for mentorship in order to help that colleague determine an achievable plan. With clear objectives, your questions can be tailored to elicit insights that align with that person's goals. Thoughtful reflection before that conversation significantly increases the likelihood that the conversational objectives are fulfilled.

Central to this preplanning is thinking through thoughtful questions in advance. Thoughtful questions are scaffolding for meaningful conversations. Instead of relying on generic topics or inquiries, take time to craft questions that prompt reflection, invite deeper sharing, and stimulate introspective responses. I mean, aren't we tired of talking about the weather? This type of question goes beyond the surface and encourages individuals to express their thoughts, feelings, and perspectives more fully. Again, this significantly increases the likelihood that your conversation will be meaningful to both you and the other person.

For example, in a one-on-one conversation with a team member, you could start by exploring his experiences with and in the team and ask him to identify his aspirations for personal growth. Questions can include the following: "Can you share a specific moment in your career with us that you found particularly impactful?" "How do you envision your role evolving in the next few years?" "Where would you like to see improvement?" "What do you perceive are milestones in your pursuit of your goals?" These questions prompt reflection and invite the individual to articulate his or her aspirations and goals.

Without question, strategic conversations rooted in thoughtful planning foster a culture of engagement. When individuals enter discussions with a clear understanding of their objectives and with well-crafted questions, the conversation becomes a collaborative exploration rather than a mere exchange of information or a superficial chat. Such dynamics promote active participation and a sense of shared purpose.

Imagine a committee or board meeting at church where the objective is to make a critical decision. With a thoughtful plan, the meeting can be structured to include perspectives from different team members, ensuring that everyone's input is considered, and to guide the discussion toward strategic resolution or defined action items. This is much more effective than merely coming to that item in the agenda and asking, "So, what do we think?" Instead, with preplanning, the result is a collaborative process that values diverse viewpoints and results in a decision.

Additionally, thoughtful and planned questions in advance of conversations are pivotal in relationship-building. Whether in personal or professional settings, the intentional planning of conversations demonstrates a genuine interest in others. When individuals feel heard and valued, a foundation of trust is established, paving the way for more meaningful and enduring relationships.

Not long ago, I had the privilege of making a home visit to someone who had been visiting our church. Her name is Emma, and she had attended church with her adult son and daughter-in-law. From information she had provided to us, I knew she was in her mid-eighties. I also knew from conversations with her that she had a very strong, distinctive German accent.

Curious about her life experiences, I brainstormed questions to ask her. And boy, am I glad I did!

Consider with me which conversation you would most like to be a part of: *Option A:* We talk about her apartment building, the weather, her health, and our church. *Option B:* We talk about her experiences in Germany in the 1940s, what it was like to come to America, what it was like to be an immigrant, and what she learned from it all. I went with Option B, of course. And what a memorable visit!

And not only did I love talking with her, but I think she did as well! People generally love talking about themselves, their experiences, and their personal histories. Thoughtful, preplanned questions help bring all this out, resulting in healthy and strengthened relationships. Our time felt like it went so, so quickly, and I have to believe Emma felt heard, cared for, and loved, and best of all, she was beautifully receptive as I shared the love of Jesus with her. It was a win all around!

I had a similar experience during breakfast with the athletics director of a large local high school. He is a member of the church I serve. Before our time together, I thought about what his role entails and what makes it challenging. In my mind, I identified some questions I could ask to help draw out this information. And what a conversation we had! I learned so much about leadership, management and communication expectations, facilitating change, working through conflict, and more! Again, thoughtful, preplanned questions helped bring all this out, resulting in healthy and strengthened relationships. Our time felt like it went so, so quickly, and I believe this person felt heard, cared for, and loved. It was a double win!

To put this into practice, I made a change in my routine that you might find helpful as well. I spend a fair amount of my time driving between home visits, hospital visits, and other appointments. For many years, I used this time to listen to podcasts, something I found enjoyable (and still do!). But after years of this habit, I found that listening to a podcast and then quickly trying to transition into serious conversations wasn't my best move. So I made a change. Now I use the travel time between appointments to plan out and think through the upcoming conversations. I use this time to prayerfully brainstorm what being open, curious, and inquisitive is going to look like in my next conversation. I have found this to be exponentially helpful. (Either that, or I call my mom. I love you, Mom!)

A quick word on where thoughtfulness and preplanning are most important: before conversations and meetings when elevated tension or conflict is anticipated. Generally, the greater the anticipated level of conflict, the more prayer, thoughtfulness, and preplanning needs to be done. These are not conversations that you want to walk into unprepared or without having given much thought. Some questions to consider:

- **How would I describe the position of the other person(s)?**

- **What leads him or her to take this position or have this understanding?**

- **What emotions is he or she feeling?**

- **What emotions am I feeling?**

- **What questions could I ask to increase understanding on all sides?**

And the beauty is, if you don't know the answer to some of these questions, guess what you can do? Use your time together to ask!

Here I suggest a little exercise. Life's circumstances often force us to do some waiting, and often, we wait in proximity to others. We might be waiting on a sideline for a sports practice to be over, at a restaurant hostess station until our table is ready, or in a waiting room at a doctor's office. Often, these moments are marked by a bunch of folks staring at their phones and scrolling.

What if, instead of scrolling, you found a person to talk to? What if, instead of talking about the weather and the failure of the local professional sports team, you asked a more thoughtful and conversation-provoking question? Now I admit that I don't always feel like doing this, and if I'm a little wiped out or feeling overwhelmed, I pass on doing so. But when I seek out a conversation through a thoughtful question, I'm thankful that I did. Some of my preferred ice-breaker questions are "What's it like to be you these days?" (my favorite); "What's bringing you joy these days?"; and "What's something that you are looking forward to?"

Back to the statement that opened this chapter: "Everyone is interesting if you ask the right questions." I've found this to be true over and over again. And how fun it's been along the way to discover it!

QUESTIONS FOR
CONVERSATION AND REFLECTION

🔊 Can you remember a time when you prepared for a conversation and it resulted in an enriching and beneficial discussion?

🔊 This chapter included this statement: "People generally love talking about themselves, their experiences, and their personal histories." When have you found this to be true?

🔊 Why might preparing for a conversation that involves conflict be helpful?

🔊 What do you find yourself doing when you're waiting?

🔊 What's an example of a time when you discovered something really interesting about somebody else that you didn't previously know?

🔊 How might these conversations lead to sharing the Gospel of Jesus Christ with others?

CHAPTER
11

What do you think?
If a man has a hundred sheep,
and one of them has gone astray,
does he not leave the ninety-nine
on the mountains and go in search
of the one that went astray?

JESUS; MATTHEW 18:12

LISTENING AND THE MISSION OF GOD

HOW ABOUT A few questions to begin this chapter and to get you thinking just a bit? Imagine that you were sent to a foreign land as a Christian missionary. Imagine that it was an entirely different land with a new-to-you culture—one you knew very little about. You were sent by your congregation as an ambassador for the purpose of sharing your faith with the people in that region. Now here are the questions: What strategy would you take? What would be your approach as you sought to reach this population? Think about that for a moment.

Wouldn't it make sense to do a whole lot of listening and relationship-building? Rather than hold a church service that would be unfamiliar to people or offer a service you didn't confirm that the people need, wouldn't it make more sense to get to know and understand the people you are attempting to reach?

Let's take it a step further and consider what questions to ask as you seek to get to know this culture—what you would want to find out. I'm guessing you would listen to people's stories, backgrounds, and experiences so you could know their values, beliefs, motivations, and opinions. And you'd probably want to know their experiences with religion, both good and bad. It would make a whole lot of sense to do a whole lot of listening.

So, if you agree with this approach as a missionary in a foreign land (perhaps you know where I'm going with this), then it makes sense to use that same tactic in an ever-changing and increasingly post-Christian world.

American culture and its attitude toward organized religion and Christianity is changing. I pastor a church in a suburban community in the Midwest, and in the fifteen years that I've been here, I've noticed a tectonic shift in how the Christian Church is viewed by our community at large. In broad strokes, it feels like the Christian Church has gone from being celebrated as a part of a community to being tolerated to being viewed with open skepticism and even hostility. The culture around us is changing; the degree of change is expanding, and the speed of change is increasing. It will likely be different from the time I write these words to the time you read them!

American culture and its posture toward organized religion and Christianity is changing, and we need to ask a whole lot of questions about it.

Take note: I don't recommend that we fight culture, taking a combative us-against-them tone. Nor do I recommend that we flee, give up, retreat, and enclave. That's not the answer either. The incarnational nature of the ministry of God in Jesus shows us that's not the way. Instead, I recommend that we ask a whole lot of questions. Like missionaries in a foreign land, we need to learn much more about the community and culture we are seeking to reach.

A number of years ago, I heard a story that has stayed with me. It's the story of a church consultant who was hired by a congregation to help them grow and reach out to their community. The consultant told the church to gather some leaders and meet him in the church lobby on a Sunday morning fifteen minutes before the start of the worship service. The leadership team expected the consultant to use this time to share insights on how the Sunday worship service feels—things like parking, seating, and the guest experience. But the consultant had a different idea. Once they were gathered in the lobby, he told them to get in their cars in groups and ride around town. They went to sports fields, coffee shops, restaurants, and local parks. Want to guess why? This was the very audience the church was seeking to reach. It would make sense to get to know who they were and what they were doing—to get in their mindset.

In chapter 3, we introduced the heart of the ministry of Jesus as the one who comes "to seek and to save the lost" (Luke 19:10). Both verbs are important. Jesus not only seeks; He also saves! He pursues. And as Jesus has done for us, we follow His example and endeavor to do the same. Since Jesus actively seeks, we actively seek. And no doubt, seeking involves listening. It's not making all kinds of assumptions or judgments about culture. Rather, it is seeking to learn its hurts, worries, dreams, and so much more, all with the knowledge that the Gospel of Jesus is the answer for the lost.

Lesslie Newbigin was a well-known twentieth-century missionary and evangelist to India. After nearly four decades in India, it was time for Lesslie and his wife, Helen, to return to their native England. He had left England in 1936 and returned in 1974. Can you imagine how different their homeland was after nearly forty years? When they returned to England, Newbigin and his wife saw that so much had changed not only in appearance but also in the hearts and minds of the people. After some time at home in England, Newbigin began to share some interesting observations. He noted that while he was in India, there were very few followers of Jesus, so the church looked and acted a certain way in order to reach the people there. Similarly in England, there were now very few followers of Jesus, but the church still looked and acted as though it was in a Christian culture. Newbigin then led a movement to help the Christian Church in Europe recognize that it ought to accept and act as though it were in a mission field.

The United States is a mission field, and we need to act as such! Seeking, listening, and asking thoughtful, conversation-provoking questions will be key habits and practices to employ in order to reach this current culture. To take it a step further, how the church-at-large views and interacts with those who think or behave differently than how the church has historically is a growth area for sure.

Although it has become all too easy to lump everyone who makes certain decisions or has a specific ideology into one bucket, with the help of the Holy Spirit, we can resist the ways of the world and the wiles of the devil to turn our backs on those who are misguided or who have rejected the church. Whether it's in the area of political beliefs, gender, sexuality, or any host of other issues, there is much room for listening, as our Lord Jesus did in His earthly ministry. Without question, the Christian should speak where the Word of God has clearly spoken. Here is a guiding principle for how we do that:

> **But in your hearts honor Christ the Lord as holy, always being prepared to make a defense to anyone who asks you for a reason for the hope that is in you; yet do it with gentleness and respect.** (1 PETER 3:15)

Listening and asking thoughtful, conversation-provoking questions is a great way to show gentleness and respect. But in the hustle and bustle of our fast-paced world, where information flows incessantly and attention spans wane, the art of listening is a rare and invaluable skill. Nevertheless, in the matter of spreading the Gospel and introducing others to the transformative work of Jesus Christ, listening is not just a skill; it is a sacred duty. Before we can share the Good News of Jesus with others, we must first listen well and ask good questions.

In the Gospel of Matthew, Jesus implores His disciples, "He who has ears to hear, let him hear" (Matthew 11:15). He tells them to listen to the message behind the words and grapple with what that message means for them. In this account, they are grappling with the fact that John the Baptist had prepared the way for the Messiah and that the Messiah was standing before them. In other words,

Jesus tells them that they have ears, so they should use them! Pay attention! This message is important!

Listening goes beyond the physical act of hearing; it extends to understanding and empathizing with the struggles, doubts, and joys of others. Before we can effectively communicate the message of Jesus, we must first tune in to the unique story of each person's life.

Every person carries a narrative, a story woven with threads of experiences, challenges, victories, defeats, and hopes for the future. Listening provides us with the key to unlock these narratives, allowing us to step into the shoes of another and appreciate the intricacies of his or her journey. As we listen, we gain insights into their hurts and struggles, creating a bridge for the Gospel to meet them precisely where they are.

In the process of attentive listening, we break down the barriers that often hinder authentic communication. People are more receptive to the message of hope and redemption when they feel genuinely heard and understood. As ambassadors of Christ, our determination to listen becomes a powerful tool to dismantle preconceived notions and skepticism, creating a space where the seeds of faith can take root.

Listening is not a passive endeavor; it is an active engagement with the stories and emotions of others. One of the most effective ways to demonstrate our commitment to understanding is through the art of asking good questions. Thoughtful inquiries not only reveal our genuine interest but also open doors to profound discussions about faith.

Good questions can probe beneath the surface to delve into the depths of a person's beliefs, fears, and aspirations. By asking about a person's worldview, values, and experiences, we invite him or her to reflect on the foundational aspects of his or her life. This process not only enriches our understanding but also provides an opportunity to share how the Gospel satisfies and fills our deepest yearnings.

Asking good questions fosters an atmosphere of trust and openness. In a world inundated with judgment and criticism, a nonjudgmental inquiry can serve as a balm to a wounded soul. Creating moments where free expression is celebrated allows individuals to express their doubts and uncertainties, paving the way for a more nuanced and compassionate presentation of the Gospel.

In the summer of 2023, church research specialist Barna Group released some compelling data on this issue. Specifically surveying non-Christians, the Barna Group researchers asked about their relationships with Christians. First, researchers asked if the survey participant knew a Christian. Then the researchers asked if that person had ever talked about spiritual matters with him or her. While this data was interesting, what I found most compelling was where the Barna Group went next. The second section of the survey invited the non-Christians to imagine a relationship with a Christian that they would be interested in learning from. They then asked which characteristics described such a person. Think for a moment about what attributes you would expect a non-Christian to desire in a friend who believes in Jesus as Lord and Savior. Would he or she want the Christian to be knowledgeable?

The clear answer non-Christians look for in a conversation with Christians is that they "listen without judgment." Interesting, right?[6]

Being present goes beyond physical proximity; it involves a genuine empathetic connection with the joys and sorrows of those around us. When we adopt this posture of presence, we communicate a profound truth—that God is not a distant deity but a compassionate friend who understands our struggles. This understanding lays the groundwork for a more receptive audience when we eventually share the Gospel.

As followers of Christ, we strive to embody the listening heart of Jesus. Jesus listened to the cries of the broken, the doubts of the skeptical, and the hopes of the weary. In our journey to introduce Jesus to others, we would do well to emulate His compassionate listening, recognizing that our role is not merely to speak but to connect with the hearts of those who desperately need the life-changing power of the Gospel.

Think about it. The Gospel is not a mere set of doctrines; it is a living and transformative message that meets people in their brokenness and leads them to redemption. However, for this transformation to occur, individuals must first recognize their need for a Savior. Listening and leading people to authentic reflection is the catalyst for this realization.

As we listen to the narratives of others, we discern their heart's cry for meaning, purpose, and fulfillment. The Gospel addresses these profound longings, offering a narrative of hope and redemption that transcends the temporal struggles of life. By understanding the specific needs of individuals, we can tailor our message to speak directly to the core of their spiritual hunger.

In the process of sharing the Gospel, we must recognize and celebrate that it is the Holy Spirit who convicts and transforms hearts. Our role is to be obedient vessels attuned to the leading of the Spirit as we engage in conversations with others. Through prayerful listening and discernment, we align ourselves with the divine work of drawing individuals into a life-changing relationship with Jesus.

In the journey of sharing the Gospel and introducing Jesus to others, listening is not a mere preliminary step; it is the very heartbeat of authentic communication. Through the ministry of attentive listening, we discover the unique narratives of individuals, identify the cries of their hearts, and create a pathway for the transformative message of Jesus.

One of my favorite examples of this is the apostle Paul and his mission work in the book of Acts. Paul's visit to the city of Philippi specifically comes to mind. In Acts 16:11–15, we see Paul engage in conversation with Lydia. By the power of the Holy Spirit, Lydia comes to saving faith in Christ Jesus, all because Paul, with the help of the Holy Spirit, went to the people in these communities, listened to them, built relationships with them, and shared with them the hope found only in Jesus Christ.

As we embark on this sacred journey, let us remember the words of James 1:19: "Know this, my beloved brothers: let every person be quick to hear, slow to speak." In our efforts to proclaim the Gospel, may we be quick to listen, recognizing that it is through the power of attentive ears and empathetic hearts that the seeds of faith find fertile ground with the help of the Holy Spirit. While the call to listen is clear, implementing effective listening strategies in our daily lives requires intentionality and practice. Part IV of this book will do just that!

QUESTIONS FOR CONVERSATION AND REFLECTION

- What approach would you take if you were a missionary in a foreign land?

- How have you seen the posture of the culture toward the church change where you live?

- Do you agree with the idea that the United States is a mission field?

- How does asking thoughtful and conversation-provoking questions help you get to know someone you are seeking to reach with the Good News of Jesus?

- How does asking thoughtful and conversation-provoking questions show gentleness and respect?

- How might taking the approach described in this chapter help plant the seeds of faith?

CHAPTER

12

Is a lamp brought in to be put under a basket, or under a bed, and not on a stand?

JESUS; MARK 4:21

TAKE A CUE FROM COLUMBO

ONE OF MY favorite television characters of all time is LAPD homicide detective Lieutenant Columbo from the long-running series *Columbo*. I remember my grandmother watching it, and it seems like a whole generation of television viewers smile when the series is mentioned. Many aspects of the title character made the show so memorable—his disheveled appearance, his beater of a vehicle, his trusty dog companion. But he was mostly known for his ability to stealthily build relationships with the perpetrators of the crimes, which, over the course of each episode, caused them to let their guards down and eventually be apprehended. In every episode, you knew who committed the crime, but you didn't know how Columbo was going to catch the person. And take a guess at what Columbo was really good at, the skill that led him to build relationships?

Lieutenant Columbo was really, really good at asking questions.

As easy as it is to dismiss this example because it's a fictional character, it's worth noting because it is a powerful, memorable illustration of an important point: thoughtful, conversation-provoking questions rooted in genuine curiosity are much more effective in relationship-building and are much more likely to lead to changed beliefs, values, and decisions than merely stating facts or opinions. That's a mouthful, I know, and a lot to process, so read it a few times and let it soak in. Do you agree with that statement? Is it the case in your life?

I've heard this described elsewhere as the "paradox of power." There's a lot to it, but fundamentally, the paradox of power states that the more you push somebody in one direction, the more likely that person is to push back the other way. Think about a time when you felt like someone was trying to convince you of something or to do something. If you are like most, your natural human response to this might have been skepticism and defensiveness. This is the paradox of power—that the more someone is feeling forced, the more likely he or she is to stay locked into his or her position.

That leads me to say this—and this may seem strange at first, but bear with me and be open to it: if you want to see a change in the life of someone else, the least effective strategy is to tell that person what to do. If you want someone to think differently, behave differently, or make a certain decision, the paradox of power says that telling that person what to do will back him or her into a corner of defensiveness. Instead, I suggest taking a cue from Lieutenant Columbo and asking thoughtful, conversation-provoking questions. Because of their power to spur self-reflection and personal examination, questions are a much more effective approach.

As well-known as Martin Luther King Jr. was for his speeches, his underlying approach to effecting change was inviting those in positions of power and authority to rethink their views. Rather than stooping to embarrass or humiliate those who thought differently than him by exposing the fallacy in their arguments, King understood human nature and the paradox of power.

The transformative power of questions surpasses the impact of statements. By embracing the habit of inquiry over instruction, we embark on a journey that not only spurs self-reflection but also nurtures an environment conducive to change and growth.

Sinful human nature exhibits a fascinating phenomenon—resistance to being told what to do. Whether rooted in a desire for autonomy or a natural aversion to coercion, individuals often bristle when confronted with explicit directives. This resistance forms a barrier that impedes the flow of genuine communication and inhibits the receptivity of the listener. Sinful humanity, tainted from birth (see Psalm 51:5), is a stubborn people!

Telling others what to do, even with the best intentions, can trigger a defensive response. The more we push someone in a particular direction, the more likely he or she is to resist and push back. This resistance not only hampers the effectiveness of our message but may also very likely sow seeds of resentment and opposition.

Humans have an innate desire for autonomy and self-determination. When individuals feel coerced or dictated to, this need for autonomy often prompts a defensive reaction. Recognizing and respecting this fundamental aspect of human psychology is crucial in fostering open and receptive conversations.

In contrast to directives, thoughtful and open-ended questions serve as a gateway to self-reflection and discovery. By inviting people to explore their thoughts, feelings, and motivations, we empower them to engage in a process of introspection that can lead to genuine transformation.

Open-ended questions encourage people to delve into the depths of their experiences and beliefs. Instead of providing ready-made answers, such questions prompt reflection, inviting people to consider the implications, nuances, and fallacies of their own perspectives. When we ask questions rather than issue commands, we transfer a sense of ownership and responsibility to individuals. The process of answering open-ended questions allows people to take agency in their own lives, fostering a sense of control and self-determination. I've seen and felt this firsthand, and I'm guessing you have as well. Additionally, asking questions cultivates a collaborative spirit in conversations. It transforms dialogue from a one-sided directive into a shared exploration of ideas and possibilities. This collaborative approach creates a space where individuals feel heard, valued, and respected.

Understanding the psychology of influence is essential in navigating conversations that inspire change. Statements, even well-intentioned ones, can trigger resistance and defensiveness. Questions, on the other hand, engage the cognitive processes of reflection and introspection, opening the door to receptivity and understanding. By posing probing questions, we guide others to examine the foundations of their beliefs, fostering a deeper understanding and a willingness to consider alternative perspectives.

Curiosity, discussed in depth previously, builds a bridge in communication, connecting individuals through a shared exploration of ideas. When we approach conversations with genuine curiosity about the thoughts and experiences of others, we create an environment where questions become invitations to embark on a journey of mutual discovery. How exciting and enthralling these conversations can be!

Meanwhile, assumptive statements, even those grounded in good intentions, can create a chasm of misunderstanding. When we assume we know what is best for someone else and assert our perspectives without invitation, we risk alienating rather than connecting. Sometimes assumptive questions can even be presented as questions, even though they are questions with implied or assumed answers. Questions rooted in genuine curiosity, however, break down assumptions, paving the way for authentic understanding.

Take, for example, when a friend or family member comes to you for advice. While we may have an initial instinct for a course of action, asking guiding questions that provoke that person's honest reflection and decision-making, rather than merely sharing our opinion, will be more impactful long-term. Let's briefly unpack this.

Asking guiding questions requires finesse, sensitivity, and a genuine, selfless interest in the well-being of others. As we explore the dynamics of guiding conversations, we discover the delicate balance between providing a framework for reflection and allowing individuals the freedom to arrive at their own conclusions.

Effective guiding involves creating a space for people to reflect on their beliefs, values, desires, and choices.

By posing questions that encourage contemplation, we provide a platform for them to explore the depths of their own thoughts and emotions.

In the process of guiding, we recognize the power of choice that people possess. Rather than imposing our perspectives, we galvanize them to make informed decisions based on their own values and aspirations. This acknowledgment of autonomy strengthens the foundation for lasting change.

Each person's journey is unique, according to God's design for his or her life. Effective guiding requires a personalized approach. By tailoring our questions to the individual, we demonstrate a genuine interest in his or her story, which fosters a connection that goes beyond generic advice or directives.

The synergy between active listening and questioning forms the heartbeat of transformative conversations. These two elements, when employed harmoniously, create a dynamic exchange that deepens understanding, nurtures empathy, and lays the groundwork for positive change.

Active listening is the soil in which the seeds of effective questioning take root. When we listen attentively, we gain insights into the nuances of a person's narrative, allowing us to pose questions that are not only relevant but also deeply meaningful to his or her experiences. Questions, in turn, serve as bridges between understanding and action. They guide conversations from passive reception to active engagement, prompting individuals to consider the practical implications of their beliefs and choices. The dance of active listening and questioning involves a fluid exchange of ideas, emotions, and perspectives. Rather than a rigid structure, this process follows the natural ebb and flow of a conversation, adapting to the distinctive rhythm and dynamics of each interaction.

Take, for example, a mentoring relationship in a work setting. In a mentoring relationship, a seasoned professional employs the art of asking questions to bridge the generational gap with a younger mentee. By asking about the mentee's goals, aspirations, and challenges, the mentor creates a space for open dialogue and mutual understanding. The mentee, feeling valued and heard, experiences a transformative journey of self-discovery and professional development. You might imagine that this is far more impactful than the mentor merely telling the mentee what to do!

This approach also works in more personal relationships. In a marriage, trust is enhanced and growth is advanced when a spouse refrains from issuing ultimatums or directives and instead employs open-ended questions to understand the underlying issues and arrive at solutions. By fostering a climate of honest communication, the couple engages in a collaborative exploration of their needs and desires. Through this process, they discover common ground and implement positive changes that strengthen their relationship.

Mastering the art of asking questions is a skill that improves with practice and intentionality. While the art of asking questions is a powerful tool, it is not without challenges. People may still exhibit resistance or defensiveness, particularly if they perceive questions as veiled attempts to manipulate or control. Understanding and addressing these challenges is essential for maintaining the integrity and effectiveness of questioning as a communication strategy. Transparent communication is crucial in addressing concerns about manipulation or hidden agendas. Clearly communicate your intentions in asking questions—emphasize a desire for mutual understanding, collaboration, and personal growth. This transparency builds trust and dispels potential apprehensions.

In the symphony of communication, questions emerge as partners, guiding individuals through the intricate steps of self-discovery, understanding, and growth. By choosing inquiry over instruction, we embrace a philosophy that respects the independence and agency of others. The transformative power of questions lies not only in their ability to provoke discovery in others but also in their capacity to illuminate the path of self-reflection. As Socrates is said to have commented, "I cannot teach anybody anything. I can only make them think."

QUESTIONS FOR
CONVERSATION AND REFLECTION

- Think back to a time when someone was trying to convince you to do something or think a certain way and it didn't feel right. Why do you think it felt that way?

- What's an example of a thought-provoking question that helped you change your mind or course of action?

- What power do questions have that assertive statements do not?

- How might this chapter impact your work relationships?

- How might this chapter impact your personal relationships?

- What do you think Socrates meant by "I cannot teach anybody anything. I can only make them think"? Do you agree with him? (It's okay to disagree!)

- How might taking this approach facilitate conversations that lead to talking about Jesus and matters of faith?

QUESTIONS FOR
CONVERSATION AND REFLECTION

PART IV

The Habits of a Listener

CHAPTER
13

The mind, once stretched by a new idea, never returns to its original dimensions.

ATTRIBUTED TO RALPH WALDO EMERSON

TRY SAYING THIS

HAVE YOU EVER experienced a new environment that made you feel lost, out of place, and unsure where to turn—but then you found a map? Whether at a park, a monument, or a shopping mall, when I see that map with a big red dot and an arrow that says "You are here," I feel like I have a better handle on what to do next. I guess it's the little things that make a big difference!

Similarly, when I'm visiting a new city, I love finding a website or travel app that instructs me, "If you only have one day in this city, be sure to do this!" It's helpful to know from an expert what I should do. Not too long ago, my family and I visited Nashville. We were directed to a specific bus tour followed by a great chicken sandwich restaurant. To top it all off, we went to a bakery that makes the best doughnuts I've ever had! We experienced all of it because of the recommendation, "Be sure to do this!"

The phrase "good listening skills" can be ethereal and abstract, and I don't think that's very helpful. Instead, I strive to be like the travel map, the helpful guide that says, "Be sure to do this!" That's why I believe we get better, and more comfortable, as a listener by practicing certain phrases or statements that inspire conversation. Some of these phrases may feel awkward and uncomfortable to say at first. They were for me. But then I saw firsthand that they worked, and now they are a part of the rhythm of my communication. Now I use them without even thinking, and it sure doesn't feel awkward anymore. It just works.

Let's start here: to truly grasp the intricacies of another person's narrative, we must go beyond hearing words to actively engaging with the emotions, nuances, and layers beneath the surface. In this chapter, we will study the significance of employing specific phrases as part of active listening. These phrases build bridges, inviting individuals to share more as they explore their emotions and feel truly heard.

Thoughtful listening is not a passive reception of words; it is an intentional and engaged process that involves both the mind and the heart. Specific phrases are tools, allowing us to navigate the landscape of emotion and experience with sensitivity and empathy. By incorporating these phrases into our conversations, we create a space for deeper understanding and connection.

Before diving into the specific phrases, it's essential to understand the heart behind thoughtful listening. Cultivating a listening heart involves a commitment to be fully present in the moment, to set aside judgment, and to prioritize the feelings and perspectives of the speaker. When we approach conversations with a genuine desire to understand, the impact of our words becomes profound. We unpacked this in chapter 9.

It may sound obvious, but it's worth saying: human experiences are a tapestry woven with both perceptions and emotions. While perceptions provide the framework, emotions color the canvas, adding depth and dimension to the narrative. The phrases explored in this chapter serve as a dance between perception and emotion, guiding conversations toward a holistic understanding of the speaker's journey. Let's get practical!

"Tell me more about that."

The simplicity of this phrase belies its transformative power. By inviting individuals to expand on their thoughts, experiences, or concerns, we signal a genuine interest in their narrative. This open-ended prompt encourages a more comprehensive sharing of information and emotions.

Asking someone, "Tell me more about that," encourages the person to examine the details and nuances of his or her story. It communicates that his or her perspective is valued and that the conversation is not bound by time constraints. This phrase opens the door to a more thorough exploration of the speaker's experiences.

Finally, this phrase is so very powerful because it shows genuine interest in the other person. It's the exact opposite of interrupting and inserting your own opinions or experiences. As we discussed in chapter 9, genuine interest is a cornerstone of thoughtful listening. When we use this phrase, we communicate that we are not seeking a mere superficial understanding but are genuinely curious about the intricacies of the speaker's thoughts and feelings. This curiosity lays the foundation for a deeper connection.

"Those are the facts, but how did this make you feel?"

Facts provide the scaffolding of a story, but emotions are the paint that brings it to life. Acknowledging the emotional dimension of a narrative enhances our understanding and demonstrates a commitment to empathetic engagement. By acknowledging the facts and then specifically addressing the response, we create space for people to express the impact of their experiences on their emotional well-being. This dual acknowledgment allows for a more holistic comprehension of the speaker's journey.

I've found that sometimes people can get stuck in their first impressions, almost like quicksand. As a thoughtful listener, be on the lookout for the balance between facts and emotions. If you sense what a person is saying is strongly facts-heavy, ask a question that gets to his or her emotions. Getting to a person's emotions might be what leads to an ultimate breakthrough.

Additionally, validation of emotions is a powerful aspect of thoughtful listening. When we inquire about emotions, we validate the significance of feelings in shaping an individual's response to an event. This validation fosters trust and encourages the speaker to share more openly.

"Let me see if I have this correct." *"Let me see if I understand."*

Clarification is an integral part of thoughtful listening. These phrases not only ensure that we accurately grasp the details of the speaker's narrative, but they also convey a commitment to precision and understanding. These phrases show that you are genuinely curious and want to get it right.

These simple phrases are helpful when trying to avoid making false assumptions. Misunderstandings can arise when we assume that we have grasped the full scope of a person's story. By using this phrase, we communicate a willingness to set aside assumptions and seek clarity directly from the speaker. This active engagement minimizes the risk of misinterpretation. At times, when I have used this phrase, I have found that I had it wrong, which then allowed the person I was talking to and me to keep talking until I got it right!

When we take the time to confirm our understanding, we affirm the speaker's perspective and signal that his or her words are significant. This affirmation builds rapport and establishes trust.

"So if I could summarize."

Summarizing is a skill that distills the essence of a conversation, capturing key points and sentiments. This phrase not only demonstrates thoughtful listening but also offers an opportunity for correction and clarification. It's similar to "Let me see if I have this correct" or "Let me see if I understand" but has added value in that summarizing what you've heard is more than merely ensuring you have the facts correct. It's an indication that you understand the heart of the matter.

Said in a different way, the act of summarizing condenses information into digestible portions, allowing the speaker to confirm or adjust the summary. This process ensures that both parties are on the same page so the conversation can move forward with a shared and accurate understanding.

Additionally—and this is what I love most about this phrase—summarizing prompts reflection for both the speaker and the listener. It encourages the speaker to consider the overarching themes of his or her narrative, while the thoughtful listener gains insight into the focal points that resonate most deeply. This reflective aspect enhances the depth of the conversation.

"Would you say that you're feeling _____?"

Directly inquiring about emotions provides individuals the opportunity to articulate and explore their feelings. This question not only invites a more nuanced discussion; it also encourages emotional intelligence because it prompts individuals to delve into their emotional states, encouraging self-awareness. By identifying and expressing their feelings, individuals gain clarity on their emotional responses and pave the way for further exploration of their experiences. Asking people to be more in touch with what they are feeling can truly help them understand their present reality.

By clarifying emotions, we demonstrate empathy and an honest effort to understand. This communicates that we are attuned to the nuances of the speaker's narrative, creating a space for shared emotional experiences. It shows genuine, thoughtful listening and builds trust.

"It sounds like you _____."

Mirroring the speaker's sentiments with this phrase validates his or her emotions and provides an opportunity for confirmation or adjustment. This reflective approach enhances understanding and establishes a connection based on shared emotional resonance.

Mirroring involves restating or paraphrasing the speaker's words, which demonstrates active listening and validation. When we reflect what we perceive the speaker is feeling, we offer an opportunity for that person to confirm or correct our interpretation, reinforcing the authenticity of the conversation.

Take, for example, a person sharing a series of hardships at work. After thoughtful listening, a reply from you might be as simple as this: "It sounds like you are feeling really mistreated at work." While that phrase may seem elemental, I've found it often results in exclamations of "Exactly!" or "Totally!"

By suggesting a potential emotional response, we invite the speaker to explore the resonance of that emotion within his or her own experience. This shared emotional experience creates a bridge between speaker and listener, fostering a deeper connection.

"What I hear you saying is _____."

Similar to the suggestions above, this phrase encapsulates the essence of thoughtful listening. By summarizing the speaker's message, we not only affirm our understanding but also provide an opportunity for the speaker to refine or expand on his or her thoughts. When we articulate what we hear, we confirm our understanding of the speaker's narrative. This affirmation reassures the speaker that his or her message has been accurately received, fostering a sense of trust and openness.

The act of summarizing invites the speaker to contribute additional insights or nuances that may not have been explicitly expressed. This collaborative refinement deepens the conversation and enhances our grasp of the speaker's perspective. Sometimes, when a speaker hears the summary from a thoughtful listener, it moves the speaker to rethink or reconsider his or her approach.

PUTTING IT ALL TOGETHER

While each specific phrase plays a unique role in thoughtful listening, the true power of such phrases lies in their interplay within the context of a conversation. Employing these phrases strategically enhances the flow of dialogue, creating a dynamic exchange that goes beyond superficial communication.

Initiating a conversation with open-ended statements like "Tell me more about that" sets the stage for a more expansive sharing of thoughts and feelings. These questions provide the speaker with the freedom to express themselves without constraints. They show genuine care and interest.

As the conversation progresses, phrases like "Those are the facts, but how did this make you feel?" bridge the gap between information and experience. This transition allows for a more holistic exploration of the speaker's narrative.

The phrases "Let me see if I have this correct"; "Let me see if I understand"; and "If I could summarize" serve as checkpoints in the conversation. They ensure clarity and provide opportunities for the speaker to confirm or refine his or her message. This iterative process enhances mutual understanding.

Additionally, phrases like "Would you say that you're feeling _____?" and "It sounds like you _____" consider into the emotional landscape, inviting the speaker to articulate and reflect on his or her feelings and conclusions he or she has drawn from them. This exploration deepens the connection between speaker and listener.

Finally, the phrase "What I hear you saying is _____" serves as a capstone, summarizing the essence of the conversation. This affirmation not only reinforces the listener's understanding; it also opens the door for additional insights and reflections from the speaker.

BONUS: TWO MORE TO TRY

It's so simple, almost too simple, but I've seen it work firsthand. The simple phrase "What else?" can pack a punch.

"What else?" shows, first, that you recognize there is more to the narrative and genuinely want to hear it. Again, it's the opposite of interrupting with an opinion or personal anecdote.

Second, it challenges the speaker to go further and deeper in his or her reflection. On one occasion in my life when I shared an experience and was asked, "What else?" I was moved to unpack a ton of stuff I never quite realized before. It was true for me that below the surface was something more significant, and all it took to uncork it all was the question "What else?"

Finally, I've heard it said this way: the first answer is rarely the only or best answer. It might take asking "What else?" to discover more.

One more question that I'd love for you to use when you're trying to fast-forward the relationship-building process came to me from author Mark Yarhouse: "Pretend like your life is a book, and I'm coming into the seventh chapter. Tell me what I've missed so far."[7] I find this to be a great question when I'm trying to go deeper in a relationship with someone I don't know that well. It might be a new coworker, a new extended family member, a new neighbor, or the like. As we say with some other questions, this one shows that you are open, curious, and genuinely interested in getting to know this person. People love to talk about themselves, and this question invites them to do just that!

Thoughtful listening is an attitude, a mindset, and a posture, no doubt. We saw it first, and most beautifully, in biblical accounts of Jesus. Now, having been changed by the power of the Gospel, we seek to share this approach with others. And it's made easier when we employ specific phrases that help us show others that we care. Now that you have several questions to ask, the next chapter will introduce a listening framework. This framework uses an acronym, which makes it memorable—and it works. Let's keep going!

QUESTIONS FOR
CONVERSATION AND REFLECTION

- Which sample phrase is most intriguing to you?

- What do these phrases have in common?

- Think of someone you speak with a lot—say a spouse, a sibling, or a parent. Does that person express more perception in his or her conversations or more emotion?

- What about you? Are you more objective in your communication or more emotional?

- What do you think is helpful about the phrases that force summaries?

- Homework time: pick a phrase to try out in a relationship in the next few days. Which one are you going to use? Why?

CHAPTER
14

But in your hearts honor Christ the Lord as holy, always being prepared to make a defense to anyone who asks you for a reason for the hope that is in you; yet do it with gentleness and respect.

PETER; 1 PETER 3:15

THE READ APPROACH

HAVING LAID THE foundation for listening as a posture, a mindset, and an attitude, and having provided some sample phrases to employ in active, engaged conversation, this chapter offers you an overall strategy and road map for thoughtful listening. It uses an acronym, which makes it memorable, for four steps to take as a thoughtful listener. Each step is important, but each step won't take equal time. In fact, the first two steps might be rather long, while the final two might be quite quick. But this strategy—Reflect, Emotion, Affirm, Disclose, or READ—is a helpful and effective approach for these conversations.

The READ Approach emerges as a compass, guiding us through the realms of understanding, empathy, and meaningful connection. This chapter will unravel the layers of this thoughtful listening strategy and explore how the elements work together to transform conversations into discoveries and growth.

In a world saturated with noise, the ability to listen thoughtfully is a rare and invaluable skill. The READ Approach is not merely a method; it is a philosophy that invites us to engage with others in a way that goes beyond surface-level communication. Let us embark on a journey through the four elements of the READ Approach, each contributing to the depth and richness of our conversations.

REFLECT

The first element, "Reflect," invites us to cultivate a reflective mindset. It urges us to pause, absorb, and then echo to the speaker what we have heard until both speaker and hearer are certain of accurate understanding. This reflective process involves using statements like "Let me see if I understand," as discussed in the preceding chapter, which fosters clarity and reduces the risk of misinterpretation.

Reflection is not a mere repetition of words; it is a process of understanding. It involves the careful navigation through the speaker's narrative, ensuring that every nuance and subtlety is captured. This active engagement lays the groundwork for trust and establishes a foundation for more profound communication.

The skill of clarification is a hallmark of reflective listening. By employing statements like "Let me see if I have this correct," we create an opportunity for the speaker to correct or elaborate on his or her message. This iterative process minimizes the potential for misunderstandings and promotes a shared understanding.

Warning 1: This first step may very well be the longest. It's going to involve hearing a lot of background and experiences. Fight the urge to interrupt; just be focused as a thoughtful listener on hearing his or her story. After listening well, provide a summary and reflective statements, as discussed in the previous chapter.

Warning 2: Do not move to the second step until you have heard from the speaker that you totally and completely understand his or her predicament. You should ask clarifying questions and provide summarizing statements until you hear the speaker share that you grasp his or her meaning. You'll know when the speaker feels truly heard and understood, as it's a relief to him or her, and he or she will let you know! At this point, you can move to the second step.

EMOTION

The second element, "Emotion," directs us beyond the facts to the heart of the matter—the emotions underlying the narrative. Thoughtful listening involves not only acknowledging emotions but also actively seeking them out and articulating them to confirm our understanding.

Emotional intelligence is a vital component of the READ Approach. By identifying and expressing the emotions tied to a story, we navigate conversations with heightened sensitivity. This emotional depth fosters a more profound connection and allows us to respond with empathy and compassion.

More often than not, emotions lurk beneath the surface, waiting to be revealed. This step in the READ Approach encourages us to create a safe space for emotional expression by using statements that invite individuals to share their feelings. By doing so, we honor the emotional landscape of the speaker's experience.

In this step, we use questions like "How did that make you feel?" and "Is it fair to say that you felt _____?" These questions help move the sharer beyond the facts and into the emotions he or she is feeling. For example, when a person is sharing difficulties at work, it's common to focus on the behaviors of a boss or coworkers. While important, until we get to the emotions that result from these actions, these folks will likely stay stuck. This step ensures that the emotions are identified.

Emotions, especially intense ones, can pose challenges in conversation. When faced with a person exhibiting strong emotions, we should approach the person with sensitivity and empathy. Using statements like "It seems like this is very emotional for you" acknowledges and creates space for the expression of feelings.

A quick word on this: not everyone is proficient at identifying their emotions, especially in the midst of difficult situations. Thankfully, helpful aids exist to help in this regard. I highly recommend Dr. Marc Brackett's Mood Meter. This color-coded chart, recently turned into a smartphone app called How We Feel, is valuable in naming and identifying emotions. I've used this with adults, children, firefighters, and even on myself!

AFFIRM

The third element, "Affirm," transcends the transactional nature of communication. It invites us to affirm something positive about the other person or the approach he or she is taking. This affirmation is a powerful tool for building and strengthening relationships.

Affirmation is a catalyst for positive change in the dynamics of a conversation. By acknowledging and appreciating specific aspects of the speaker, we create a climate of respect and mutual understanding. This positive reinforcement creates an environment where individuals feel valued and heard. I've found it often lowers the emotional temperature in the room and reduces high-energy negative sensations.

Integrate affirmations into conversations with mindfulness and sincerity. Look for genuine and God-pleasing aspects to affirm, whether you're affirming a person's strengths, efforts, or positive approaches. This intentional affirmation builds a culture of positivity and respect.

Finally, affirming something about the other prepares the heart of the speaker for what is to come next, our fourth element. You are an ally to the speaker—someone who is in his or her corner. Think about it. This person is coming to you for help likely because something is wrong. This often results in a self-esteem deficit. Your affirming words play a role in reshaping the person's internal narrative and prepares him or her for what comes next.

DISCLOSE

The final element, "Disclose," encapsulates the culmination of thoughtful listening. After investing time and energy in reflective understanding, empathizing, and affirming, we seek permission to share our insights and perspectives.

This gentle unveiling is grounded in respect and a genuine desire to contribute positively to the speaker's journey.

Disclosing requires a delicate balance of discernment. Before offering feedback or insights, we consider the impact our words may have on the individual. Thoughtful listening equips us with the discernment to choose the right moment and the right words for disclosure.

Seeking permission to disclose is a sign of respect for the other person. It acknowledges that the person's story is his or her own, and any contribution we offer is by invitation only rather than an imposition. This mutual understanding enhances the receptivity of both people.

It may sound like this: "Thanks for sharing all of this. If I have some feedback, are you in a place to hear it?" Or this: "Thanks for sharing all of this. Would you be open to me sharing some of my thoughts about it?"

The bottom line is that we are putting the ball in the speaker's court, making him or her much more likely to receive it well. After all, he or she asked for it!

Thinking of this step, I cannot help but think of this verse:

> **But in your hearts honor Christ the Lord as holy, always being prepared to make a defense to anyone who asks you for a reason for the hope that is in you; yet do it with gentleness and respect.** (1 PETER 3:15)

I've found this approach can work in a number of environments.

In a workplace setting, tensions arise between two team members. When the READ Approach is used, a mediator listens thoughtfully as each person shares his or her perspective. After sharing reflective statements to ensure understanding, emotions are unveiled, affirmations are offered, and permission is sought to disclose insights. The resulting conversation becomes a collaborative exploration, leading to resolution and improved team dynamics.

Within a family facing conflicts, a member employs the READ Approach to foster understanding. Reflecting on each family member's perspectives, acknowledging emotions, and affirming positive aspects of his or her approach, the individual creates a foundation for a more open and supportive family dynamic. The thoughtful disclosure of personal insights is met with receptivity, contributing to family harmony.

A friend faces personal challenges, and thoughtful listening becomes a source of support. Reflecting on the friend's experiences, expressing empathy for her emotions, affirming her strengths, and seeking permission to share insights, the listener navigates the complexities of the friend's journey. The disclosure is received with gratitude, deepening the friendship bond.

Here's a quick story that you might find helpful. Several years ago, a mom in our church with health challenges underwent major surgery. Because her husband traveled a great deal for work, her situation took quite a toll on the family, especially on the oldest child. On a home visit following the surgery, I wanted to talk with not only the recuperating mom but also the stressed and overworked oldest daughter. As I prepared for this visit, I realized (thanks be to God) that merely speaking face to face with the teenage daughter wouldn't get me very far. I mean, who wants to talk extensively with their pastor, especially a teenager? I knew I needed to take a different approach.

On my way to the visit, I picked up a few ingredients to make a quick dessert. After visiting with the mom, I invited the oldest daughter, who is quite creative and artistic, to help me for a few moments in their kitchen. There, we made the dessert together.

While we made the dessert, she talked about what the experience had been. Not just the reality of the situation, but her emotions underneath it all. I got a chance to affirm her, her love for her mom, and all she was doing, and I got a chance to remind her to keep working hard at school too! It was a much easier conversation to have shoulder to shoulder than face to face, if you know what I mean.

Thankfully, the READ Approach served as a great road map. Let me encourage you to give it a chance and watch it work!

QUESTIONS FOR
CONVERSATION AND REFLECTION

- Why is it important that we ask clarifying questions until proper understanding is achieved?

- Have you had an experience where you felt accurately heard and understood? How would you describe it?

- Why is naming and identifying the emotions underneath it all so critical to listening thoughtfully?

- Why is it sometimes hard or confusing to properly identify our emotions?

- How would you describe the role affirmations play in thoughtful listening?

- When has someone disclosed helpful feedback to you?

- Where do you think the READ Approach might be most useful in your life?

CHAPTER
15

And if you greet only your brothers, what more are you doing than others?

JESUS; MATTHEW 5:47

FOR WHEN YOU DISAGREE

I HOPE YOU are starting to practice some of the strategies in this book and that you're seeing positive results. In the remaining pages, we will drill down into two specific arenas and circumstances where thoughtful listening is especially difficult to practice.

The first is this: thoughtful listening in situations that are laden with conflict. In the crucible of conflict, where emotions are heightened and passionate opinions diverge, the art of thoughtful listening emerges as both a shield and a bridge. This chapter delves into the profound importance of listening well during times of discord, emphasizing that as tension increases, the need for thoughtful listening becomes even more critical. The overarching goal in these challenging moments is to listen to those who think differently until we can articulate their beliefs to their satisfaction, fostering understanding and contributing to the resolution of conflicts.

Conflict is an inherent aspect of human interaction. It's fueled by differences in opinions, values, personal histories, and perspectives. Whether in personal relationships, professional settings, societal debates, or even in churches, conflicts arise. In the midst of these tensions, thoughtful listening acts as a helpful catalyst, unraveling the threads of misunderstanding and paving the way for resolution.

As tensions escalate, the impulse to speak and assert our own views often intensifies. However, the counterintuitive truth is that the higher the level of tension, the greater the need for thoughtful listening. That's so important. Can we read that again? *The higher the level of tension, the greater the need for thoughtful listening.* In moments of conflict, thoughtful listening becomes a strategic imperative, offering a pathway to de-escalation, understanding, and constructive dialogue.

The ultimate goal in times of conflict is not merely to hear the words of those with opposing views but to internalize and understand them to such an extent that we can articulate them to the satisfaction of the other person. This goal requires an active engagement with the perspectives and reasoning of others, even when they stand in stark contrast to our own.

I credit and give thanks to God for this approach as being a huge part of how the congregation I serve navigated COVID-19. As you likely remember, this was a hugely emotional time, as fear and uncertainty seemed to reign. Two schools of thought emerged around it, and in the midst of all of it, our congregation made a lot of difficult decisions. Our church leadership, as a slice of culture as a whole, had folks who thought quite differently about how best to respond. For quite some time, meetings and conversations were heated and conflicted. And then, we experienced a breakthrough.

I don't remember exactly when it was, but I remember how I felt when we did it: we had a meeting where we decided to focus less on arriving at a decision and a lot more on understanding one another's positions. We took the time to let people talk and share experiences and opinions. In doing so, people felt valued and heard. This enabled us to get to the root of where people were, which made it exponentially easier to arrive at consensus and agreement. Thoughtful listening in the throes of severe conflict worked wonders, glory to God!

In the context of conflict, thoughtful listening operates as a dynamic force that shapes the contours of conversations. This multifaceted approach involves reflective, empathetic, and strategic elements, each contributing to the overall efficacy of communication.

REFLECTIVE LISTENING IN CONFLICT

Reflective listening in conflict involves unraveling the layers of misunderstanding by summarizing and restating the views of the other person. This process not only clarifies the person's perspectives but also signals a genuine commitment to understanding. Through reflective listening, we build a foundation of mutual comprehension that can withstand the pressures of disagreement.

In these moments, you'll want to use some of those summarizing phrases we learned earlier, such as "Let me see if I understand you correctly" and "Is it fair to say that you feel _____?" A good benchmark is to commit to not moving on to expressing your opinion until you get a resounding sense from the other person that he or she feels heard and accurately underwood.

In times of conflict, assumptions and misinterpretations abound. Clarification, achieved through thoughtful listening, becomes a powerful tool for dismantling these barriers. By seeking confirmation and correction, we navigate the intricate web of conflicting views, fostering an environment where understanding can flourish.

EMPATHETIC LISTENING IN CONFLICT

As you've likely experienced, emotions run high in moments of conflict, and thoughtful listening extends beyond the exchange of thoughts or opinions to encompass the emotional landscape. By acknowledging and articulating the emotions embedded in differing perspectives, we bridge the gap between intellect and empathy, fostering a more comprehensive understanding.

Empathetic listening is the bridge that connects disparate viewpoints, allowing individuals to traverse the emotional terrain of conflict together. It involves not only recognizing emotions but also expressing genuine empathy for the experiences and perspectives of others. In heated conflict, this is admittedly not easy, but it is essential.

In the midst of conflict, empathy becomes a catalyst for connection. When we convey an understanding of the emotional impact of differing thoughts and opinions, we create a shared space where individuals feel heard and valued. This emotional resonance forms the foundation for collaborative problem-solving.

My observation is that conflict often fosters an us-versus-them mentality, deepening divisions and hindering resolution. It's what we see normed in culture, so it seeps into our communities and institutions. Empathetic listening disrupts this dichotomy by humanizing the other person's perspective. By acknowledging shared emotions and experiences, we break down barriers and pave the way for common ground.

STRATEGIC LISTENING IN CONFLICT

Strategic listening in conflict is the intentional effort to internalize and understand opposing views to such an extent that we can articulate them accurately and convincingly. This strategic approach transcends the immediate exchange, aiming for a deeper level of comprehension that contributes to conflict resolution.

Strategic listening goes beyond the pursuit of agreement; it aspires to a level of understanding where we can articulate the beliefs of others with clarity and authenticity. This depth of understanding lays the groundwork for collaborative solutions and minimizes the risk of misrepresentation.

To put this into practice, conversations that involve conflict would do best to include moments where each party is challenged and invited to restate and articulate the position of the other party. This would, in ideal scenarios, include not just surface-level understandings but also the why and the emotions behind and underneath it all.

Similarly, the strategic use of silence becomes a powerful tool. Allowing moments of quiet reflection communicates a genuine commitment to understanding rather than a rush to rebuttal. Strategic silence provides space for thoughtful consideration and reinforces the importance of the other person's perspective. Sometimes, these moments involve a race to talk over one another. Strategic silence, meanwhile, are set-aside moments to pause, lower the temperature, slow down, and reflect. Silence becomes a canvas for reflection, enabling both parties to absorb and process the complexities of the conversation.

Amidst the tensions of conflict, a crucial rule of thumb emerges: monitor your percentage of talking in the conversation. The guideline is clear—aim to speak no more than 50 percent of the time, or ideally, less! This rule serves as a practical anchor, preventing conversations from becoming dominated by one voice and ensuring that thoughtful listening remains at the forefront.

BEST PRACTICES FOR IMPLEMENTING THOUGHTFUL LISTENING IN CONFLICT

Implementing thoughtful listening in conflict requires intentional effort and a commitment to the principles of reflective, empathetic, and strategic listening. The following best practices offer practical guidance for navigating conversations in heated moments:

1. Practice and Model a Reflective Foundation: Before sharing and disclosing anything of your own, model first the important practice of reflecting. Try phrases like

"Let me see if I understand correctly" to ensure accurate comprehension. Establishing a reflective foundation from the outset sets a tone of openness and a commitment to understanding.

2. Navigate Emotional Terrain: Acknowledge and address emotions early in the conversation. Practice empathetic reflection by articulating not only the facts but also the emotions embedded in the other person's perspective. Use empathetic listening to recognize and validate the emotional aspects of differing perspectives. Creating space for emotional expression fosters a climate of empathy and mutual respect. Don't be afraid to attempt to name and identify the emotions present.

Use phrases like "It sounds like you're feeling _____" to express genuine empathy and understanding. This empathetic approach builds bridges across emotional divides. As the conversation progresses, strive for a level of understanding where you can articulate the other person's beliefs to his or her satisfaction. This strategic goal goes beyond agreement to achieve a depth of comprehension that contributes to conflict resolution.

3. Monitor Your Talking Percentage: Throughout the conversation, be mindful of the amount of time you're talking. Strive to keep your speaking time below 50 percent, allowing ample space for the other person to express his or her views. This intentional balance fosters an environment where thoughtful listening can flourish.

4. Employ Strategic Silence: Incorporate strategic silence into the conversation, especially during moments of tension. Resist the urge to fill every pause with words. Strategic silence provides room for reflection and underscores the importance of thoughtful consideration.

Conflict isn't easy to navigate, but thoughtful listening can be an absolute game changer in helping you get through it. Because we live in a culture and context that tends to demonize people who think differently than we do, making them "the other," moments of conflict can quickly escalate. Thoughtful listening provides a needed path forward. As my friend and author Les Stroh memorably quipped, "Conflict is inevitable. Enemies are optional."[8]

I'll close out this chapter with a memory from my days as a student at Concordia Seminary, St. Louis, when I was preparing to become a pastor. As a part of our studies, we were sent to area congregations for fieldwork experience. Occasionally, these congregations experienced conflict, and seminarian fieldwork students would sometimes get triangulated into the conflicts. To avoid this, we were invited to learn a phrase to repeat when it seemed like folks were attempting to triangulate us. The phrase was this: "I'm only a seminarian. I don't know a lot about that yet. That sounds like something you should talk to your pastor about." We actually couldn't leave for fieldwork until we had that memorized!

Thinking back to this, it may be time for us to memorize a similarly cadenced refrain for when we are in the midst of inevitable conflict. How about this: "That's interesting. I'm not sure I quite agree. But I'm glad we're friends!"

QUESTIONS FOR
CONVERSATION AND REFLECTION

- Think back to moments of conflict you've experienced. Are they often marked by how well you listened?

- What makes thoughtful listening in moments of conflict so difficult?

- Do you agree with this statement: "The higher the level of tension, the greater the need for thoughtful listening"? In what way (or ways) is this accurate?

- What role might silence play, strategically, in moments of conflict?

- Why is it tempting and common to seek to speak more than 50 percent of the time in moments of conflict? Why might asking good questions be a more productive approach?

- "Most people aren't toxic people. They just see things differently than you do." Do you agree?

- What's an example of a situation of conflict that you are in where thoughtful listening might be a blessing?

CHAPTER
16

I've regretted my speech;
never my silence.

ATTRIBUTED TO XENOCRATES

FOR THE GRIEVING

HERE'S A QUICK question to begin the last chapter: Do you prefer swimming in a lake or a pool? While I love a nice dip in a cool pool on a hot summer day, to me, there is nothing like swimming in a lake. There is something to the natural beauty and grandness of it all. My personal favorite spot is swimming in Lake Michigan while at beautiful Camp Arcadia in northwestern Michigan.

There is, however, one challenge with lake swimming, especially in smaller lakes—all the muck at the bottom of the lake! A combination of decomposing plants, algae, mud, and leaves from shoreline trees makes swimming in smaller lakes sometimes unpleasant. This muck lies under the surface, not always visible, and it's something you don't really want to step in and stir up.

I bring that up because there is "lake muck" of sorts in our lives: ungrieved, or inadequately grieved, losses we experience but don't appropriately process. Like lake muck, they are unpleasant, sometimes hidden, and something we don't care to step in and stir up.

I conclude this book with a chapter on thoughtful listening surrounding grief because just about all people deal with this one way or another. So in this chapter, we'll explore some foundational principles of Christians and grief and touch on how thoughtful listening plays a role in helping others work through it.

Although we might not realize it, grief is all over the Bible. Not only are there narrative stories where people experienced grief, such as John 11:1–44 and Luke 7:1–17, but we also see in the book of Psalms how people who were experiencing grief cried out to God. For example:

Be gracious to me, O Lord, for I am in distress;
my eye is wasted from grief;
my soul and my body also.

For my life is spent with sorrow,
and my years with sighing;
my strength fails because of my iniquity,
and my bones waste away.

(PSALM 31:9–10)

You can hear it in the voice of David, who wrote Psalm 31. He's struggling. His thoughts are consumed with anguish. He has experienced years of groaning and feels it in his body. He's grieving.

As much as we think of grief after the loss of a loved one, grief is caused by many things. It can be the loss of a relationship, a job, health, and other things. It can even be an unmet expectation, something that you longed for and hoped for but never materialized.

Also, grief doesn't have to be major to be valid. As grief has many forms and causes, it also has many levels.

Grief that's more severe for others is still real for you. For example, if I lose a friend to cancer, I may say, "I'm sad, but look at how it is for his spouse! That's much worse." While well-meaning, this minimizes the grief I feel and prevents me from processing appropriately what I am experiencing.

Over a decade ago, I lost my dad to cancer. It was a blow to my family and me. Years later, I started to realize that I hadn't grieved adequately or appropriately. I was busy pastoring a church, fathering a family, and more. I was in a rush to get to the other side of grief. Welcome to my therapy session!

Not long ago, I spoke with professional grief counselor and friend Lydia Schlueter. She shared this truth with me that I pass along to you: "Christians sometimes rush grief because of our hope in Jesus Christ."[9]

In other words, we say, "Yes, but Jesus" statements. For example, we say "Yes, I'm sad, but Jesus is my hope." Such statements are true and well-meaning but effectively force the Christian to move quickly through grief, to rush the grieving process or even communicate that "real" Christians don't grieve. Rushed grieving is not adequate or appropriate grieving and can result in significant problems down the road, like depression, anxiety, post-traumatic stress disorder, and more.

Schlueter argues that Christians need to learn to say, "Yes, and" statements that acknowledge grief as appropriate and realistic. These might sound like this: "Yes, Jesus is my hope, and I'm still really hurting." "The Gospel of Jesus Christ is my anchor, no doubt, and I'm still hurting." If you've never felt it was appropriate to say that or feel that, let me give you permission to say that today. Remember, "Jesus wept" (John 11:35).

Before we dive into what it looks like to be a thoughtful listener to the grieving, here are three truths about grief. First, healthy, active grieving deepens our relationship with our Lord. While it's unpleasant to grieve, when we lament, cry out, emote, confess to, talk to, or even question God, we are drawing near to Him. That's more than a good thing—it's what our heavenly Father wants us to do.

Second, healthy, active grieving is worked through, never dismissed. It's not something to be gotten through. It's not a race to the other side. Instead, it is best understood as something thoughtfully and patiently worked through. As tempting and somewhat appealing as it is to rush it, don't hurry to pass over the pain. Grief needs to be felt, leaned into, worked through, and not minimized.

Finally, healthy, active grieving is only done with others. During these times, we can celebrate that we are not only brought near to God but we are also brought near to others. Statistics prove, over and over again, that people who have support and grief in relationship with others grieve healthier. The ministry GriefShare has a proven track record of creating spaces where this happens. Visit GriefShare.org to learn more.

If this, then, is true, how might thoughtful listening shape how we help people who are grieving?

Grief is a weighty and universal human experience—one that necessitates a unique and delicate approach to conversation, which is why I dedicated this chapter to learning how to do it well. Fighting the instinct to help people, to fix their problems, and to quickly get them through their situation, the art of being present and allowing space for processing emotions becomes paramount.

Grief is a sacred journey, an intricate tapestry of emotions, memories, and reflections. Even in the best of circumstances, grief is complex and complicated! When someone is navigating the tumultuous terrain of loss, thoughtful listening becomes a compassionate companion. It is not a quick fix or a solution. Rather, it creates secure space where emotions can be expressed, memories can be shared, and the pain of loss can be acknowledged.

In the presence of someone else's grief, a natural human instinct to fix and to offer solutions or words of comfort that might alleviate the pain exists. However, grief is not a problem to be solved but a process to be lived. The power of presence, expressed through thoughtful listening, lies in the capacity to bear witness to the emotions, memories, and stories that unfold in the wake of loss.

Grief is a fragile state, and those in mourning often find themselves navigating uncharted emotional territory. Thoughtful listening acknowledges this fragility and offers a safe place where individuals can express their grief without fear of judgment or the pressure to conform to societal expectations of how grief should be experienced.

The Jewish tradition of "sitting shiva" provides a poignant metaphor for the role of thoughtful listening in the context of grief. Shiva involves a period of mourning during which friends and family gather to offer support and companionship to the bereaved. This practice aligns with the essence of thoughtful listening, emphasizing presence, empathy, and a willingness to bear witness to the pain of loss.

During shiva, the emphasis is on presence rather than solutions. Similarly, in thoughtful listening during times of grief, the focus is on being there for the grieving individual, offering a comforting and nonjudgmental presence. It is an acknowledgment that grief does not have a quick fix, and sometimes, the most profound support comes from the simple act of being with someone in his or her pain.

Thoughtful listening creates a sacred space for grief to unfold. It is a space where the bereaved can speak openly about their loved ones, share memories, express anger or confusion, and, most importantly, feel heard and understood. This sacred space is not about imposing one's own beliefs or solutions but about allowing the unique journey of grief to unfold organically.

Navigating the grief of another requires a unique set of skills in communication. The art of thoughtful listening in this context involves a combination of empathy, patience, and a deep respect for the grieving individual's unique experience.

Empathy, rooted in the love that the Lord Jesus first showed us, is the cornerstone of thoughtful listening in grief. It involves not just hearing the words spoken but also connecting with the emotions behind them. Thoughtful listeners recognize and acknowledge the pain, sadness, anger, and confusion that may accompany grief. Through empathetic listening, they create a space where these emotions can be expressed without judgment.

Every individual's grief journey is unique. Thoughtful listening involves acknowledging and respecting this uniqueness. Instead of offering generic condolences or platitudes, it entails recognizing that each person's relationship with the deceased—and thus his or her experience with grief—is distinct.

Grieving individuals may experience a range of emotions that fluctuate unpredictably. Thoughtful listening involves responding to these emotional nuances with sensitivity. It may mean being a supportive presence during moments of intense sadness, providing space for anger or frustration, or sharing in moments of laughter when memories bring joy.

Additionally, grief follows its own time line, and there is no predetermined schedule for healing. Most important here is that it cannot be rushed or forced. Thoughtful listening requires patience—a willingness to allow grief to unfold at its own pace. This may involve multiple conversations over an extended period, as well as understanding that certain anniversaries or triggers may bring renewed waves of sorrow.

Grief is not a linear process but a journey with its own ebb and flow. Thoughtful listening recognizes that the impact of loss extends beyond the immediate aftermath and requires ongoing support. It involves being present for the long arc of grief, understanding that healing is a gradual and nonlinear process.

In the realm of grief, silence can be as powerful as words. Thoughtful listening involves embracing moments of quiet reflection and allowing the grieving individual the space to simply be without the pressure to fill every pause with conversation. Silence becomes a sacred language, communicating understanding and companionship.

Thoughtful listening in grief is grounded in respect for the individual's coping mechanisms. Some may find solace in sharing stories and memories, while others may prefer moments of solitude. Thoughtful listeners respect these preferences, understanding that there is no one-size-fits-all approach to grieving.

Thoughtful listening refrains from prescriptive language that imposes specific ways of coping. Instead of saying, "You should . . ." or "You need to . . . ," it involves statements like, "How can I best support you right now?" or "What would be most helpful for you right now?" This open-ended approach respects the autonomy of the grieving individual. It's thoughtful listening at its best.

This is, after all, the approach Jesus takes with Mary and Martha as they mourn the loss of their brother, Lazarus, in John 11:1–45. They had listened to His teaching and believed in His resurrection promise. Now He shows up for them and allows them to emote and grieve. He is present with them when they need Him the most. He hears their prayers and answers those prayers out of love and mercy for them.

This, then, is a beautiful, full-circle way to conclude this book. This book is centered on the compassionate approach Jesus takes in relationships, which we would do well to emulate. Jesus tells us to "love one another: just as I have loved you, you also are to love one another" (John 13:34). This command, this imperative, rests on every

Christian. Jesus fulfilled it in perfect obedience to the heavenly Father that we may know love, grace, forgiveness, mercy, and hope of eternity with Him. And because He laid down His life for us, we can open our ears and hearts to others so that they may know His responsive heart and transformative love.

In a closing scene for you, I'm at a rooftop restaurant with my daughter Megan. I love her dearly. Despite all of our family busyness, we had a moment to finally catch up. She is talking, almost nonstop, about what is going on in her life: the drama, the highs, and the lows. At some point, I interject, "Do you want some feedback on this?" Her reply is about as I expected:

"No, I just want you to keep listening."

QUESTIONS FOR CONVERSATION AND REFLECTION

🗩 How have you experienced grief?

🗩 Did you find yourself wanting to rush through it?

🗩 Who in your life helped you and was present with you as you experienced grief?

🗩 How is "sitting shiva" a helpful model for walking alongside the grieving?

🗩 Why are humans so tempted to want to "fix" the grieving?

🗩 Can you think of a time when you were helpful and present with someone who was grieving?

🗩 What principles of thoughtful listening discussed in this book will be helpful when you are with someone who is grieving?

🗩 What have you learned about Jesus' approach to asking questions that will help you point others to the reason He took this approach— to reveal Himself as our Redeemer and Savior?

END NOTES

1   "Revealing Average Screen Time Statistics," Backlinko (website), March 11, 2024, https://backlinko.com/screen-time-statistics (accessed May, 22, 2024).

2   Tomas Laurinavicius, "Screen Time Statistics 2024: Average Usage of Mobile, Social Media & TV," *Marketful*, April 9, 2024, https://bestwriting.com/blog/screen-time-statistics/#:~:text=The%20average%20screen%20time%20in,16%20minutes%20on%20mobile%20devices (accessed May, 22, 2024).

3   Brian K. Davies, *Connected to Christ: Overcoming Isolation through Community* (St. Louis: Concordia Publishing House, 2021), 11–12.

4   *Luther's Works*, vol. 35, p. 258.

5   Pauline Ashenden, "Nonverbal Communication: How Body Language & Nonverbal Cues are Key," Lifesize (website), February 18, 2020, https://www.lifesize.com/blog/speaking-without-words/#:~:text=These%20studies%20led%20Dr.,is%20%E2%80%9Cnonverbal%E2%80%9D%20in%20nature (accessed May 22, 2024).

6   "What Are People of No Faith Looking for in Faith Conversations?" The Barna Group (website), July 19, 2023, www.barna.com/research/no-faith-conversations (accessed May 31, 2024).

7   Mark Yarhouse, "Understanding Gender Dysphoria," February 4, 2016, YouTube video, https://www.youtube.com/watch?v=0_l_grc5lmk (accessed May 22, 2024).

8   Les Stroh, conversation with the author, February 22, 2024.

9   Lydia Schlueter, conversation with the author, June 15, 2023.